KU-592-545

# FIVE DAYS WHICH
# TRANSFORMED RUSSIA

THE
SECOND
WORLD

# The Second World series

*Series editor* Teodor Shanin
Professor of Sociology, University of Manchester

## Already Published

THE CHALLENGE: ECONOMICS OF PERESTROIKA
Abel Aganbegyan

THE PEOPLES OF THE SOVIET UNION
Viktor Kozlov

RURAL RUSSIA UNDER THE NEW REGIME
Viktor Danilov

## Forthcoming Titles

IS THERE A FUTURE FOR THE WARSAW PACT?
Oleg Bogomolov

SEMIOTICS OF CULTURAL HISTORY
Yuri Lotman

THE SOCIAL DIMENSION OF THE PERESTROIKA
Tatiana Zaslavskaya

4 0008195

# FIVE DAYS WHICH WHICH TRANSFORMED RUSSIA

## Sergei Mstislavskii

Translated by Elizabeth Kristofovich Zelensky
Introduced by William G. Rosenberg

R.T.C. LIBRARY LETTERKENNY

947 0841

THE
SECOND
WORLD

Hutchinson
London   Melbourne   Sydney   Auckland   Johannesburg

Hutchinson Education

An imprint of Century Hutchinson Ltd
62—65 Chandos Place, London WC2N 4NW

Century Hutchinson Australia Pty Ltd
PO Box 486, 16—22 Church Street, Hawthorn,
Victoria 3122, Australia

Century Hutchinson New Zealand Limited
PO Box 40—086, Glenfield, Auckland 10,
New Zealand

Century Hutchinson South Africa (Pty) Ltd
PO Box 337, Bergvlei, 2012 South Africa

First published 1923
© English translation, Hutchinson Education, 1988

Set in 11/13½ pt Parlament Roman
Printed and bound in Great Britain by
Anchor Brendon Ltd, Tiptree, Essex

British Library Cataloguing in Publication Data
Mstislavskii, Sergei
　　Five days which transformed Russia.—(The
　　Second World).
　　1. Russian Revolution, 1917-Personal observation.
　　I. Title.　II. Series.
　　947.084'1'0924

ISBN 0 09 173034 1 (cased)
　　　　　0 09 173094 5 (paperback)

# CONTENTS

List of Maps and Plates vii

Akcnowledgements viii

*Foreword to* The Second World: *Teodor Shanin* ix

Introduction: *William G. Rosenberg* 1

**1 The First Day** 17

THE FEBRUARY RISING
27 February — 1 March 1917

**2 The Second Day** 57

THE FOUNDING OF THE PROVISIONAL GOVERNMENT
3 March 1917

**3 The Third Day** 79

THE ARREST OF NICHOLAS II BY THE PETROGRAD
 EXECUTIVE COMMITTEE
9 March 1917

**4 The Fourth Day** 109

THE OCTOBER REVOLUTION
25 October 1917

**5 The Fifth Day** 133

THE DAY OF THE CONSTITUENT ASSEMBLY
5 January 1918

Glossary: *Jonathan Aves* 157

*Plate 1*  Armed revolutionaries, October 1917

# LIST OF
# MAPS AND PLATES

**Map**

Street map of Petrograd, 1917       xii/xiii

**Plates**

 1   Armed revolutionaries       vi
 2   Revolutionary Military Committee leaflet       xiv
 3   Revolutionary soldiers       16
 4   Red Guards, Petrograd       41
 5   Michael V Rodzianko       58
 6   Aleksander Fedorovich Kerensky       69
 7   Nicholas II       78
 8   Russian soldiers       91
 9   Kronstadt sailors       108
10   Factory meeting       121
11   Sverdlov, Chernov, Martov, Spiridonova,       132
     Lenin, Trotsky
12   Revolutionary soldiers and sailors       145

# ACKNOWLEDGEMENTS

The publishers would like to thank the following for permission to reproduce photographs:-

BBC Hulton Picture Library: Plate 11 (bottom right); Fotokhronika Tass: Plate 9; John Massey Stewart Photo Library: Plates 1, 2, 3, 5, 6, 7, 8, 10, 11, (exc. bottom left and right) 12 ; Mary Evans Picture Library: Plate 4.

# FOREWORD TO
# THE SECOND WORLD

'In the West they simply do not know Russia . . . Russia
in its germination.'

*Alexander Hertzen*

As a publication project *The Second World* pursues an explicit
goal, admits to a bias and proceeds on a number of assumptions.
This should be stated at the outset. The series will aim to let the
Soviet authors and their historical predecessors in tsarist Russia
speak with their own voices about issues of major significance to us
and to them. It will focus particularly on their explorations of their
own society and culture, past and present, but set no rigid boundaries
to these; some of the texts will be more general while others will
carry primary evidence, for example, memoirs, documents, etc.
Many of the texts have been commissioned to reflect the most
recent efforts and the controversies of Gorbachev's *perestroika*.

To bridge differences of culture and experience each of the
books will carry a substantial introduction by a Western scholar
within the field. Particular care will also be taken to maintain
satisfactory standards of translation and editing.

A word about words. A generation ago the term 'Third World'
was coined in its current meaning, to indicate a somewhat
imprecise combination of societal characteristics — the post-
colonial experience, under-industrialization, relative poverty and
the effort to establish an identity separate from the superpowers,
the 'Bandung camp'. This left implicit yet clear which were the

other two 'worlds'. It was 'us' and 'them', those best represented by the USA and those best represented by the USSR. Much has changed since, giving the lie to crude categorizations. But in research and the media, at the UN and on television, the words and the meanings established in the 1960s are still very much with us. This makes the title of our project intelligible to all, yet, hopefully, should also make the reader pause for a moment of reflection.

Turning to the invisible rules and boundaries behind our editorial selection let us stress first the assumption of considerable social continuity between pre-revolutionary and post-revolutionary societies. Present without past is absurd (as is, of course, the treatment of the USSR as simply the Russia of old). Next, to talk of pre-revolutionary Russia/USSR is not simply to talk of the Russians. The country is multi-ethnic, as have been its intellectual achievements and self-evaluations. Yet all the books presented are deeply embedded in Russian language and cultural traditions. Lastly, we shall aim to show Russia/USSR neither as the 'goody' nor as the 'baddy' but focus attention on the characteristics particular to it.

*The Second World* is biased insofar as its choice of titles and authors consistently refuses the bureaucratized scholarship and paralytic tongue which has characterized much of the Soviet writing. In other words, it will prefer authors who have shown originality and courage of content and form.

Western perceptions of the Soviet scholarly achievement, especially of its social self-analysis, have usually been negative in the extreme. This was often enough justifiable. Heavy censorship stopped or biased much Soviet research and publication. 'Purges' have destroyed many of the best Soviet scholars, with whole disciplines closed on orders from above. The Soviet establishment has excelled in the promotion of safe scholars — the more unimaginative and obedient, the faster many made it into the limelight. However, much of the hostile detachment of the Anglo-Saxon scholarship and the media originated in its own ideological bias, linguistic incompetence and a deeper still layer of mutual miscomprehension. To understand the human experience and thought in a particular social world, one must view it on its own terms — that is, with full awareness of its context — of history, political experience, culture and symbolic meanings. This necessitates the overcoming of stereotypes rooted in one's own experience and a challenge to the most persistent prejudice of all — the belief that everybody (and everything) is naturally 'like us', but somewhat less so (and that the best future mankind can have is to be like us but even more so).

The bafflement of the mainstream of Western scholarship at the dawn of Gorbachev's reforms has accentuated the collective miscomprehensions of Soviet society. On the one hand stand those who see nothing happening because nothing can happen: 'totalitarianism' is not open to any transformation from within. On the other hand stand those to whom the USSR is at long last becoming 'like us'. Both views miss the most important point, that Soviet society is moving along its own trajectory which can be understood only on its own terms. This makes the need to allow this society and its scholars to speak to us in their own voice, an urgent one.

Uniformity and uniformization are false as perceptions of history and wrong as social goals, but so also is any effort at keeping human worlds apart. This is true for international politics, scholarly endeavour and daily life. Half a century ago a Soviet diplomat, Maxim Litvinov, a survivor of the revolutionary generation which was then going under, addressed the League of Nations to say: 'Peace is indivisible.' The World War to follow did not falsify this statement, but amended it. Peace proved divisible but only at the heavy price of human peril. The same holds for knowledge.

*Teodor Shanin*
*University of Manchester,*
*Great Britain*

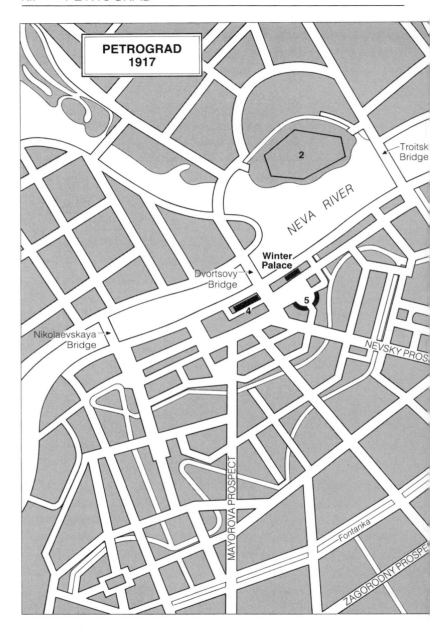

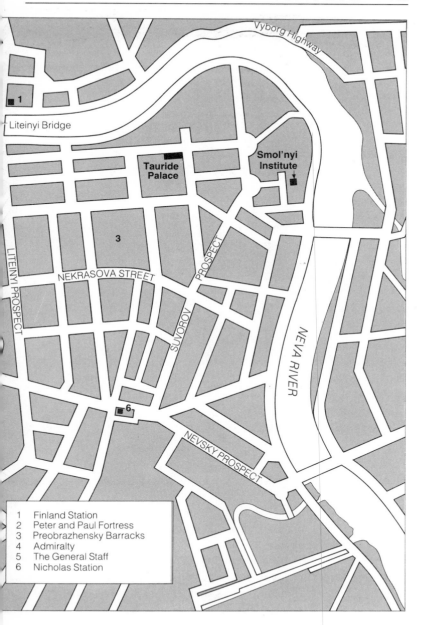

1   Finland Station
2   Peter and Paul Fortress
3   Preobrazhensky Barracks
4   Admiralty
5   The General Staff
6   Nicholas Station

Plate 2   Leaflet issued by Revolutionary Military Committee, November 1917

The Revolutionary Military Committee of the Petrograd Soviet of Workers' and Soldiers' Deputies

To the Citizens of Russia

The Provisional Government is deposed. The state power was taken over by the organs of the Petrograd Soviet of Workers' and Soldiers' Deputies Revolutionary Military Committee which leads the proletariat and the garrison of Petrograd.

The goals the people struggled for — an immediate democratic peace, abolition of landownership, workers' control of production, the creation of a Soviet Government — are now secured.

Long live the revolution of workers, soldiers and peasants!

The Revolutionary Military Committee of the Petrograd Soviet of Workers' and Soldiers' Deputies
25 October 1917, 10 o'clock in the morning

# INTRODUCTION: S.D. MSTISLAVSKII AND THE RUSSIAN REVOLUTION

Although memoir literature on the 1917 revolution abounds, Sergei Dmitrievich Mstislavskii's *Five Days* provides fascinating material about five important events and a unique perspective on the mentality of the militant populist Left — the only non-Bolshevik group to join Lenin's government after October. Born S.D. Maslovskii in Moscow on 23 August 1876, he was well educated at the University of St. Petersburg and began his career as a scientist. Like many of his generation, he became active in revolutionary politics during the 'dress rehearsal' of 1905, and participated in the armed uprising in Moscow in December. A Socialist Revolutionary with strong commitments to radical reform, Mstislavskii soon distinguished himself as an outspoken champion of peasant and worker rights. His vision of the future was moulded from both broad-based populist conceptions and a sense that revolution in Russia could ultimately be successful only by means of a 'mass' alliance of workers and peasants 'from below'. During the war he became an officer of the General Staff Academy in Petrograd, serving as librarian. When the revolution broke out in February, his military position made him an important and strategic contact for the leaders of the Petrograd Soviet, and he soon put his post to good advantage as a member of the Soviet's military commission.

Mstislavskii's broad outlook, undoubtedly reflecting the views and values of many of his contemporaries, is quite clear from his memoirs. *Five Days* is pervaded by a very strong sense of the power of Russia's 'masses', garrison soldiers at first, the mobilized workers in October, the tens of millions of militant peasants at the time of the Constituent Assembly in January 1918. 'I stood there for a long time, watching their silent ranks . . . file past me. Their machine guns, carefully wrapped in felt, seemed like strange, primeval beasts. And from this noise, from the machine-gun belts, gleaming copper, criss-crossed upon their poorly clad chests, from the pure and silent thought which sprang so clearly from these hundreds of men, and which united them body and spirit into a single whole, a sudden joy came over me. Everything became light and clear again — truly Spring had come.' 'Spring', for the populist Mstislavskii, is the flowering of popular energy and spirit, the chance at last after decades of oppression to create a new and democratic social order based on freedom and the 'popular will'.

Like other members of the Russian intelligentsia who felt themselves deeply attached to the people, Mstislavskii to some extent romanticizes these 'masses': the 'wide-open eyes of workers and soldiers' are 'trusting', 'clear', 'full of anticipation', and 'almost childlike'; his military detachments will join him with the 'wave of a hand'; the victory in October is 'their first holiday, the first day of "their" revolution . . . .' What is particularly interesting about his memoirs, however, is the way they suggest he also has 'ominous forebodings' that the very childlike attributes he recognizes will ultimately prevent the revolution from creating the society of freedom and social justice he so passionately desires. His excitement in the early days of the revolt is tempered by a sober conviction that 'not enough blood has been shed', that the exultation of Soviet and government leaders is based on faith, not knowledge. By the time of the Constituent Assembly meetings in January 1918, the last of Mstislavskii's 'five days', the cries of the sailors have become 'curt' and 'abrupt', their 'pupils dilated, wound tighter than a spring'. If the power of ordinary men and women constitute the motor force of Russia's revolutionary change for Mstislavskii, he remains uncertain from start to finish how this force might organize and control itself, and best achieve its potential.

The uncertainty is quite characteristic of the broad populist orientation Mstislavskii reflects. In this view, the creation of a disciplined party and the imposition of order 'from above' is clearly not the way. From the 1870s onwards Russia's populists had suffered continuously from their inability to channel political energies and instincts into effective organization, a fault which was partly the result of their concern not to 'fetter' the popular will. Among extremists, terror was better than a broad and well-organized political movement, since conspiratorial cells could either frighten the regime into granting reform or ignite popular rebellion. *Five Days* reveals very clearly Mstislavskii's sharp contempt for political manoeuvring and politicians in general, even though he was an active Socialist Revolutionary and played an important party role. 'The revolution found us, Party members, fast asleep,' he writes, 'like the Foolish Virgins of the Gospel.' Popular action itself was clearly more important in bringing revolutionary change than *any* political move-ment, however well constructed. 'The truth of the matter was that outside the small circles stewing in their own con-spiratorial juices, or, even worse, in militaristic and patriotic ecstasies, the socialist parties of those days were completely bankrupt.' So, too, in Mstislavskii's view, were virtually all of the figures who emerged as leaders in the new government, and even in the Petrograd Soviet. 'Neither side was honest. The higher ranks of both the Council of Ministers and the Soviet of Workers' Deputies lied in equal fashion . . . .' This was largely because, in Mstislavskii's populist vision, both sides 'feared the masses' ! They were also more concerned with restoring order and 'normality' to revolutionary Russia than with giving free reign to popular instincts and desires.

Mstislavskii is ready to 'fight', as he puts it, against the 'false' leadership of the Soviet-Government alliance, even as he seems to recognize the dangers and contradictions in his hostile attitudes and passionate commitments. The deepening of social conflict is inevitable, but however brutal and bloody the fighting, he has no doubts whatsoever about which side of the barricades he must be on. If Kerensky, Miliukov, and other state figures believed deeply in 'Russia' in 1917, and committed themselves to their country 'right or wrong', Mstislavskii might be said to have believed in the Russian *people*, right or wrong, whatever the pain or suffering they might inflict. In this as in other ways, his voice in *Five Days* sounds the authentic tone of Russia's deep and fervent populist tradition.

From this perspective, the Bolsheviks were obviously not an attractive affiliation for Mstislavskii. Lenin and his comrades shared the populists' commitment to worker and peasant interests, but rejected as mindless and politically naïve their lack of attention to mass politics and the tasks of political mobilization. Mstislavskii joined instead Russia's large and rather loosely organized Socialist Revolutionary Party (PSR), the political heir to several late nineteenth century populist groups. Although formed in 1901, the party only held its first national congress in 1906, after its legalization in conjunction with the October 1905 Manifesto and the creation of Russia's rudimentary parliament, the Duma.

From the beginning the PSR was a polyglot group, kept together only by its uniform commitment to improving popular welfare, especially that of the peasants. Its Left wing included a number of terrorists and terrorist cells, as well as others who shared Mstislavskii's passionate commitment to the people, and from the start the party as a whole never rejected violence as a tactical weapon. Its early 'Combat Organization' was responsible for assassinating Sipiagin, the tsarist Minister of Interior in 1902, the Minister of Internal Affairs Plehve two years later, and others. On the party's

Right were men like N.D. Avksentiev and V.V. Rudnev who rejected terror, and who worked to bring the PSR into the mainstream of Russian political activity. Attempting to balance these two tendencies were the party's prominent 'centrists', the best known of whom was Victor Chernov, later the Provisional Government's Minister of Agriculture. As Oliver Radkey notes in his well-researched history of the party in 1917, the organizational tasks of Chernov and the PSR centrists were virtually hopeless. Their unenviable position left them constantly exposed to bitter attacks from both flanks.[1]

The tsarist regime's extremely brutal policies of repression in the countryside after 1905 threw the party into new disarray. So did its efforts under P.A. Stolypin to break up the old commune and create a nation of hearty, individual, farmsteads. Political activism in the villages became extremely difficult, even as PSR members felt it increasingly urgent. The party was deeply committed to the nationalization of land and the socialization of agrarian production, not the creation of individual property rights and ownership. The core of its programme, formally adopted at the First Congress in 1906, demanded the expropriation of all privately held estates *without* compensation, and their redistribution along with state domains for the use of the peasants. Russia instead now seemed to be moving in just the opposite direction, destroying in the process what PSR members regarded as the socialist essence of Russia's communal culture and traditions. For some, the problem warranted a return to the tactics of terror and assassination; for others, a retreat to legitimate parliamentary forms. Factions grouped around *Revoliutsionnaia Mysl* ('Revolutionary Thought') and *Znamia Truda* ('Labour's Standard'), and members on each flank split off to form new groups, the Maximalists (*Maksimalisty*) and the Popular Socialist Party. The result was greater ideological confusion and organizational disarray, a condition the PSR had not overcome by February 1917.

Perhaps the most divisive issue, however, and the one which

most distinguished Mstislavskii and others after 1914 from their PSR comrades to the centre and right, was the war. Like other European socialist parties, the PSR had initially taken a strong internationalist position, along with Lenin and the Bolsheviks. The solidarity of workers and peasants everywhere was thought to transcend nationalist attachments. Just as with the Social Democrats, however, the actual outbreak of war moved many in the party to the right. Avksentiev, Rudnev and others adopted a strong 'defensive war' position, while Mstislavskii, Chernov, and others continued to oppose the war altogether.

These fissures widened in 1917 partly because Lenin himself took such a strong position against the war. At the second PSR conference in Petrograd in early April, which took place just as Lenin returned to Russia with his 'April Theses', the split between Left and Centre over the war question became essentially a division between those who unequivocally supported the Soviet (which had itself adopted a 'defensive war' position), and those who tacitly allied themselves with the Bolsheviks in opposition. The role of Minister of War Kerensky — himself a former SR — in mounting the June offensive further deepened the party rift; and by the time of the seventh party council meeting in August, PSR stalwarts like Breshko-Breshkovskaia were openly accusing both Mstislavskii and Chernov of treason.

In these circumstances, the Left SRs gravitated naturally and inevitably into their own political formation, closely associated with the Bolsheviks. Mstislavskii and others rejected the views of Chernov and the Centre on continuing coalition government, and called for a unilateral socialist regime; and as popular attitudes also became more radical, so did the political outlooks of SRs elected to leadership positions in local soviets, factory councils, soldiers' committees, and similar revolutionary groups. Towards late 1917, the important Petrograd organization was almost entirely in Left SR hands, just as the Petrograd and Moscow Soviets themselves came legally under Bolshevik control. In early

October, the Left SRs met as a separate SR faction, and while still officially a part of the PSR, announced their 'coalition' with the Bolsheviks. Of the 154 PSR delegates elected to attend the Second All-Russian Congress of Soviets in October, sixteen were from the right, forty were from Chernov's rather tenuous Centre, and the remaining ninety-eight were Leftists.

Mstislavskii and others did not believe, however, that the Bolsheviks should unilaterally take power. 'We were so sure of the utter inability of the Provisional Government to offer any resistance to the transfer of power to the labouring masses', he writes, that 'we stepped forward in unambiguous and absolute opposition to Lenin's doctrine of revolt.' In this posture as in others, Mstislavskii and his Left SR colleagues blended deep populist commitment and a general aversion to practical politics into what their opponents regarded as a position of incredible naïvety. Strong proponents of class (or 'social') struggle but averse to civil war, which they regarded as 'political', they failed to perceive the natural relationship between the two, and the manner in which social conflict in general is necessarily a struggle for power. Instead, their concerns drew them 'inevitably back into the charmed circle of using the old government apparatus', in Mstislavskii's words again, 'which we had, in words at least, rejected'.

Still, when the moment came, Mstislavskii and others stood with the Bolsheviks. The break with other SRs was complete. In late November, the Left SRs held their first independent party congress, although political independence in Russia was now increasingly a fiction. Such ambiguity doomed them to weakness and even ignominy. A.L. Kolegaev, I.Z. Steinberg, and other Left SRs who joined the Bolshevik regime in November legitimized Lenin's claim that his was a coalition government broadly reflecting the distribution of party allegiances within the Soviets. Indeed, the Left SRs helped contain possible opposition to the new order from among the peasantry, at least until the Bolsheviks' decree on land (which reflected entirely the left SR position) was widely disseminated; and also from among the railway workers and the soldiers, many of whom still considered themselves SRs. In fact, the new regime was increasingly dictatorial; Lenin had no intention of effectively sharing power outside Bolshevik ranks.

These considerations were far less important to Mstislavskii himself, however, than defending the revolution and struggling in the people's name. In late October and November he played an important role in organizing detachments of Red Guards, working directly out of Bolshevik headquarters in Smol'nyi. His association with the Bolsheviks strengthened. In January 1918 he joined Trotsky and others as a member of the first Brest peace delegation; and when most of his Left SR comrades turned against Lenin to protest at what they regarded as the abandonment of internationalism after Brest-Litovsk in March, Mstislavskii continued to struggle for his cause, first in the Supreme Military Council, and then as a member of the first Bolshevik government of the Ukraine. His subsequent civil war career was equally distinguished.

At the end of the war Mstislavskii returned to his writing, preparing pamphlets and other materials for the All-Russian Council of Trade Unions, and serving as an editor of the *Great Soviet Encyclopedia*. He wrote some fiction and produced several film scripts, but his most notable piece of writing was *Five Days*, impressionistic essays on five memorable revolutionary moments in which he took an active part. His memoirs were apparently composed during 1917 and 1918, immediately after the events they describe. They subsequently appeared in 1922, published in Berlin by the journal *Letopis' Revoliutsii*.

'Day One' for Mstislavskii is really the momentous forty-eight hours between 27 February and 1 March, when the Petrograd Soviet and State Duma Committees were organized and together formed the first Provisional Government, ending 300 years of Romanov rule. As students of the Russian revolution are well aware, the immediate chain of events leading to the fall of the tsar began on 23 February,

'International Women's Day', when angry men and women waiting long hours in the cold for bread and other foodstuffs joined workers and other demonstrators to protest against shortages and conditions in general. The protesters' ranks were swelled by thousands of workers from the massive Putilov plant, locked out in a wage dispute. On 24 and 25 February, the demonstrations spread, and by 27 February engulfed the city. On that day, perhaps the most significant of the period, soldiers of the Petrograd garrison joined the protests.[2]

Mstislavskii's account of the soldiers' revolt and his descriptions of events in the Tauride Palace, where both the State Duma Committee and the Petrograd Soviet were organizing, are notable in several ways. Mstislavskii knew that large demonstrations had been taking place in the city for several days. Troops had been called out in large numbers on 25 February, and by the morning of the 27th, parts of Petrograd resembled an armed camp. On the 26th he had himself walked around the area near the garrison, and had seen the 'close-knit, reliable backs of soldiers shielding this "fortress" '. Yet when news of the shooting reached him on the 27th, he was stunned to realize that the soldiers themselves were joining the revolt.

His reaction was no doubt a typical one, and pinpoints an important and overlooked aspect of the February revolution as a whole. Many like Mstislavskii fully expected strikes and other forms of workers' protests to continue in late February 1917, as they had in great numbers for many months. January and early February had been a time of especially sharp conflict. A number of leading workers' representatives had been arrested, disputes at Putilov and elsewhere had intensified, and the mood of the Vyborg district in particular (where most of the city's metal workers were concentrated) was extremely volatile. Through it all, however, few if any expected the soldiers' loyalty to break. What was truly *spontaneous* about the February revolt, as Mstislavskii suggests, was not the strikes and demonstrations but the sudden way in which the Volyhn' Regiment and other elite units suddenly joined the workers' cause. Mstislavskii's vivid description of a crawling truck, 'so massive and awe inspiring that its gears could barely shift, bristling with bayonets and overflowing with soldiers, workers, students, and women', symbolized for him the extraordinary coalescence of social forces which had finally made the revolution.

The surprise and confusion felt by Mstislavskii was broadly shared. His depictions of the Tauride Palace are notable in part because they show so clearly how the 'leadership' of the revolution was itself running behind events on the streets, how few in positions of authority fully understood the implications of what was happening. Most expected loyalist troops from outside the city to march quickly on the capital, even if the garrison commander, General Khabalov, could not restore order. And Soviet and Duma leaders alike wondered with Mstislavskii whether 'there was truly a revolutionary atmosphere in the city', or if the days of the revolt were numbered, along with those of the mutineers. A military officer fully versed in strategy and tactics, Mstislavskii himself clearly expected the military strategy employed successfully to suppress the revolts in 1905-07 to be used again, and with similar results.

This tension partly explains the origins of 'dual power', the division of authority between the Petrograd Soviet and the newly organized Provisional Government which became the most important structural aspect of the new political order. As Leopold Haimson has argued, one of the central aspects of 'dual power' had to do with the ways in which it represented and articulated 'a sense of the deep divisions that separated the upper and lower strata of urban and rural Russia, and of the inevitability of their reflection in the institutional framework that would have to be pieced together to defend the country and the revolution'.[3] Yet Mstislavskii's memoirs also make it clear just how much the new Soviet leadership doubted its ability to withstand the expected counter-revolutionary assault without the assistance and support of the 'propertied' classes and the Duma leadership. The Soviet's decision not to participate formally in the new government, and to support it 'only in so far as' it served the interests of Russia's workers, soldiers, and peasants, was both ideologically and practically determined. And so, in Mstislavskii's view, was the 'disingenuousness' with which the new regime asked him and other radicals to serve in its ranks.

By Mstislavskii's 'second' day, 3 March, there was no longer any question of the revolution's success. Nicholas had abdicated and his uncle had refused to take the throne. Even loyalist troops had no choice but to fall in behind the banners of the new political order. The question now was how, exactly, that new order would be constituted; and here the populist Mstislavskii is at pains to argue that both Soviet and government figures were essentially hostile to the interests and aspirations of the 'masses':

> Even yesterday it had still been relatively easy to be 'representatives and leaders' of these working masses; peaceable parliamentary socialists could still utter the most bloodcurdling words 'in the name of the proletariat', without even blinking twice. It became a different story however when this theoretical proletariat suddenly appeared here, in the full power of exhausted flesh and mutinous blood . . . . They were scared. And who could blame them?

Thus the initial leadership of the Soviet, moderate Mensheviks and centrist Socialist Revolutionaries, was *not* an authentic voice of the people, in Mstislavskii's view, and shared power with the Provisional Government as much to *contain* popular radicalism in cooperation with the 'bourgeoisie' as to advance popular interests.

For Mstislavskii, setting the stage in this way is important to rationalizing the Bolsheviks' coming to power in October, an event with which, as we have seen, he and other Left SRs were not entirely comfortable. The 'cheerful' tapping of rifles awakens him on 25 October, but he is somewhat surprised that the Kronstadt sailors at his door have ignored their earlier decision not to support any Bolshevik attempt to take over the government until after the Second All-Russian Congress of Soviets. A Congress vote would certainly have authorized the change in regimes, but the decision of elected Soviet representatives would have grounded it in a semblance of revolutionary legality, and possibly avoided what Mstislavskii regarded as the 'needless' complication of rupturing all ties with other socialist and bourgeois groups. Like other Left SRs and even many within Lenin's party itself, Mstislavskii feared a unilateral takeover would be 'tantamount to suicide'. His concern here, of course, is not with legality in the Western constitutional sense of the term, but with a clear and formal Soviet mandate; and as in March, he continued to harbour fears about the power of the Right to prevent the emergence of 'a new and real (and I emphasize this word) Soviet order'.

Much that had occurred in revolutionary Russia between March and October thus seems to have convinced Mstislavskii that the takeover was 'premature'. By a 'real' Soviet order, he clearly had in mind a system of social relations and state administration based securely on representative workers' and peasants' institutions, the soviets. Eight months had been far too short a time for these institutions to be firmly established; their lines of authority were unclear, and the degree of control they actually had over the attitudes and actions of the 'masses' was extremely tenuous. The process of revolutionary change had, in effect, proceeded at different rates on several social levels, and so did a developing understanding of its meaning. At the 'top', among the *verkhi* (upper strata) of both the Provisional Government itself and the soviets' Central Executive Committee, the revolution had been directed to secure Russia's national borders against the threat posed by the Germans, both to the country's international well-being (the view of the liberals) and to the revolution itself (the view of revolutionary supporters of a 'defensive war'). 'Revolution' meant the reformation of state power and governing institutions to assure the success of both these tasks; their complementarity underlay the crucial decision to continue with the war, and especially to mount the June offensive, which the government and soviet both supported in order to bring the fighting to a successful conclusion but which ended in disaster. At the 'commanding heights', social reforms and even the creation of permanent, democratic political institutions had largely to await the re-establishment of social order, and even the end of the war in the eyes of some, if the rights of millions of men in uniform were to be fully protected. Among the *nizy*, however, the masses of ordinary men and women working in shops and factories and in the fields, 'revolution' meant little if not social betterment, an end to long-standing social grievances and economic deprivation. Workers' committees, soldiers' organizations, peasant soviets and the like sprang up quickly, partly encouraged by the regime itself. They soon took responsibility (or 'control') over local affairs. Those 'above' insisted their powers be exercised in a way that did not compromise national interests; those 'below' had difficulty distinguishing Russia's national needs from their own.

Mstislavskii fully recognizes the ways in which the revolution 'below' rapidly changed Russia's social order in 1917. He understands (and fears) the resulting social polarization and its political implications. Unlike his SR comrades to the Centre and Right, however, as well as those in other moderate socialist parties, he accepts and even welcomes the surge of radical energy from below, convinced it will eventually create a strong and effective socialist order.

Whether he eventually felt this goal was realized is impossible to say. It is clear, however, that when the Bolsheviks moved on 25 October, he saw he had no choice but to join them and hope for the best. His work in the Bolshevik-Left SR coalition and then in the new Soviet state itself testifies to his deep and long-standing populist commitments; but his description of one long meeting of the Constituent Assembly on 5 January 1918, his 'fifth' day, suggests he also had his doubts.

The Constituent Assembly had long been considered the means of creating a new constitutional order. Its convocation at the earliest possible moment was one of the first stated tasks of the government in March, but weeks went by before rules governing the election process could be worked out and preparations made for the vote. This was partly because liberals and others feared its outcome, partly because there was genuine concern that the social turmoil and especially the situation of millions of men at the front might lead to massive disenfranchisement and consequent challenges to the Assembly's legitimacy. First set for September, the elections were ultimately postponed until November 1917, and hence took place after the Bolsheviks came to power. Lenin hesitated, but soon agreed they should go forward. His concern was to minimize anti-Bolshevik sentiment, although he may also have felt that the outcome would prove more favourable than many supposed. In the end, the party fared reasonably well in Russia's cities and towns, although the overwhelming number of votes in the country at large went to the SRs. (In Petrograd, for example, they received 45 per cent of the vote, compared to the Liberals' 26 per cent and the SRs 16.2 per cent; in Moscow, the figures were 47.9 per cent, 34.5 per cent and 8.2 per cent, respectively.)[4]

It was not so much the distribution of sentiment which troubled Lenin and other Bolsheviks, however, as the constitutional form itself. Party officials allowed the Assembly to convene, again to deter unnecessary opposition, but the exercise was patently futile; and as Mstislavskii describes so vividly, impatient sailors themselves eventually declared 'That's Enough!' His description of the exhausted 'remnants of February' stumbling dejectedly into the snow, frightened, helpless, and cloaked with little more than a sense of their own dignity, suggests that he himself now shared some of their concerns about whether Soviet Russia would actually become the kind of socialist order he so deeply desired.

Mstislavskii's 'Five Days' are obviously only glimpses of Russia's extraordinarily rich and complex revolution. They are not without bias or error. Like all memoirs, they must be read with caution, as much for what they reveal about the author and the perspectives of people like him as about the process of revolution itself. Yet they are an extraordinary and unique part of the literature. Virtually alone among memoirists of the period, Mstislavskii brings the perceptions of a deeply committed revolutionary populist to the events he describes, as well as the attitudes and impressions of one who is himself an active participant. Unlike the much more controlled and self-assured memoirs of a Miliukov or a Trotsky, or the relatively detached perspectives of an observer like Sukhanov, one finds here the conflicted thoughts and feelings of one who constantly struggled to play what he thought was a proper role in the evolution of events, even as he believed, in contrast to his Bolshevik friends, that the real forces of revolutionary change were beyond his power to direct. And in contrast to the memoirs of Chernov or Kerensky, Mstislavskii has no consistent or official position to defend, only a passionate interest in the welfare of Russia's people. His writer's sense is thus acutely tuned to the drama of these five days both from the standpoint of social history, and in terms of the ways these events both justified and challenged his deeply held convictions. The scenes he sketches thus constitute a particularly interesting and vivid portrait of the way five days helped change the fate of modern Russia.

## NOTES

1. Oliver H. Radkey, *The Agrarian Foes of Bolshevism* (New York, 1958).
2. The story is told in detail by Tsuyoshi Hasegawa, *The February Revolution. Petrograd, 1917* (Seattle, 1981), and E.N. Burdzhalov, *Russia's Second Revolution: The February 1917 Uprising in Petrograd*, translated by Donald J. Raleigh (Bloomington, 1987).
3. Leopold Haimson, 'The problem of social identities in early 20th century Russia', *Slavic Review*, Spring, 1988.
4. The best English language discussion of the elections and a summary of their results is in Oliver H. Radkey, *The Elections to the Constituent Assembly* (Cambridge, Mass., 1950).

*William G. Rosenberg, University of Michigan*

*Plate 3*   Revolutionary soldiers on the march

# THE
# FIRST
# DAY

## The February Rising

27 February — 1 March 1917

Goooßtes.

'There's shooting on the drill field.'

At that first moment I couldn't believe it. Still, I got up and walked over to have a look.

The windows along the back of the staff headquarters wing at the Nicholas Military Academy faced the Suvorov parade ground. Beyond it, on the other side of a high wall and across the street, stretched the Preobrazhensky barracks, which were being used temporarily to house the reserve battalions of the Volhyn' and Lithuanian regiments.

I saw nothing unusual through the window. The cellar. The guardhouse. A woodpile. Fences. Laundry, stiff from the cold, hanging on clotheslines. As far as the eye could see the drill field was empty — ominously empty, at an hour of the morning when normally cavalry cadets would be hurrying across to the riding hall for the first practice session.

I threw on my overcoat and stepped out. The heavy double doors of the courtyard entrance were propped shut. In the courtyard the gatekeeper, unusually dishevelled and fidgety, was shifting his weight from one foot to the other.

'You'd better not go out there, your honour. They're shooting. The treasurer went out, then came back. As soon as he turned the corner they started on him, rat-tat-tat . . . from a machine gun or something.'

'But how could that be. Who could be shooting here?'

Who indeed? For this whole section of the city, along the line, the Liteinyi and Suvorov Prospects, and Basseinaya Street, overflows with barracks, military establishments, hospitals and warehouses. It is a veritable 'fortress'. When, in those long ago days of the 1900s, we as members of revolutionary organizations within the armed forces considered various plans for an armed rising, we always assumed this area to be the government stronghold — the last and strongest position for loyalist troops. So many army units were concentrated here: the Guards regiments, escort troops, the 9th Reserves, a division of gendarmes, the mounted artillery, the 1st Guards Artillery Brigade, the Preobrazhensky Regiment, the Guards Field Engineers, the 18th Field Engineers, the Military Academy, the cavalry officers' school, and many other smaller units. Revolutionary experience had taught us that troops fight much more willingly and tenaciously in the neighbourhood of their barracks — and it goes without saying, even more fiercely within the barracks themselves. Even now — during these February days, with crowds rolling across the city from one end to the other like unhindered waves — here, in our 'military district' encircled by barbed wire, quiet reigned: not one rebellious shout, not a single demonstration.

Walking in the streets only yesterday, at the height of the demonstrations on Ligovka, Znamenskaya and Liteinyi Prospect, everywhere I saw the close-knit, reliable backs of soldiers shielding this 'fortress'. Yesterday, for the first time, they fired on the crowd thronging the Nevsky Prospect. Following the volleys, the people ran from the streets. No answering shots were heard from the 'fortress'. There was no fighting. Who, and by what powers, could have broken through to the drill field today?

Then, suddenly, with the impact of a hammer's blow, came the word, so unexpected, so unlikely, which clarified everything with its one whispered sound.

'They say it's the Volhyn' Regiment which has mutinied.'
The Volhyn' Regiment?!

As soon as the heavy oak gates swung open, the irregular, untidy sound of shots fired at random became audible. Muffled, they seemed to be coming from some distance away. I walked up to the corner of the building and saw, huddled at the entrance to the Academy offices, a dozen or so porters and labourers. They hugged the wall and gazed with a mixture of fright and fascination into the depths of the courtyard at the opposite end of the drill field. There, in the distance, by the riding school and stables, by an open gate leading to the barracks of the Volhyn' Regiment, I could make out small grey figures, gathering together, then scattering apart, waving their arms up and down. Rifle barrels glinted in the sun.

One of the men in the cover of the wall motioned timidly with the palm of his hand, as though in warning. Immediately (was it by chance?) a stray bullet ricocheted mischievously off the frozen cobblestones at my feet.

I had walked no more than half the distance from the main building of the Academy to the gate when the men milling around the wall made a sudden dash for it; pushing and shoving each other, huddled together, they ran clumsily up the drive. I looked around to my right, beyond the church, where stacks of birch and pine logs stretched as far as the riding school, and there I could see the soldiers coming. They were stooping close to the ground, crouching in ditches, past heaps of garbage and behind stacks of wood, running and crawling; they had no caps and some of them no overcoats, only unbuttoned jackets. The shooting beyond the far wall, on Parade Street, became louder. I walked up the now empty drive of the Academy.

In the chancellery vestibule clerks and office workers crowded around four hussars from our squadron and a half dozen soldiers from the Preobrazhensky Regiment, all winded and breathing heavily.

A sergeant who had already made his official report was now telling the story in his own words to the officer on duty.

'They came in a band: "Out into the street," they said, "the game is up, boys." We left in a hurry, just as we were, without rifles and bayonets. They were looking for cartridges, but didn't find any. And they didn't touch the storeroom.'

'Drunk?' the colonel asked, with a sneer.

'Not a bit of it. Completely sober.'

'Did the whole squadron leave?'

'Everyone, with no questions. Except us four.'

'Much obliged to you for that. Now, what shall we do with the Preobrazhensky men?'

Soon everything became clear. When the Volhyn' Regiment mutinied, their neighbours, a company of Preobrazhensky Guards just returned from 'pacification duty', scattered in case of reprisals. They were joined by those members of the Volhyn', Lithuanian and Preobrazhensky Regiments who, in general, 'were not looking for trouble', as they later explained to us in the cellar of the Academy.

'Hardly seems right, does it — without a word, to kill the gentlemen officers . . . someone will pay for it, for sure.'

The run-aways made for our drill field, where they gathered in the riding school. Then, when the soldiers of the Volhyn'and Lithuanian Regiments broke down the gates, they ran on, to Tauride Street and the Suvorov Museum. Some of them hid in the Academy, where they had been preceded by several of their own officers.

'Can we hide them in the cellars?'

'Best be careful,' grimaced our janitor Platonich, red-haired and fox-faced. 'If they find them, they'll tear down the whole Academy. Better to put them in the printing office, in the paper store.' The office supervisor, who had wandered in, stuck out his head from behind those of the pomaded clerks and protested in a squeaky falsetto: 'The storeroom is a bad idea. The entrance to the printing office leads directly on to the drill field.' But since everyone always listens to Platonich in matters of housekeeping, the Preobrazhensky men were hidden behind the stacks of paper.

Gloom reigns in the common room of the Military Academy. The instructors even walk quietly, making sure that their spurs don't jingle. They frown. They are silent. Only one of our most ancient lieutenant-generals mutters to himself, shaking his grey sideburns stubbornly from side to side as if arguing with someone, though not one word has been addressed to him the entire evening. 'Nonsense. They'll return and repent. Where can they go? . . . Hmmm? That's precisely it . . . where can they go?' And he presses, for the sixth time, the servants' bell.

'I wonder, hmm . . . what's keeping the tea?'

Scraping the parquet floor with his spur, which had slid down over the heel, the officer on duty rushed in — a worried expression on his face. 'The Preobrazhensky soldiers have just bayoneted Bogdanovich.'

Someone crossed himself. The supply officer, our junior and quite frank in the manner of the cavalry, frowned as he gazed about at the generals' insignia, plastered on various uniforms around the room. 'Yes indeed . . . if a corporal with a head on his shoulders should happen to turn up right now, this business could turn rather sticky.'

There was nowhere to go.

The revolution found us, Party members, like the Foolish Virgins described in the Gospel, fast asleep. Now, five years later, it seems incomprehensible that we failed to feel (not to say 'recognize') in the ever mounting waves of February's disturbances, the harbinger of the approaching storm. How did it happen that for so many of us — who had been preparing for this very day through long tsarist years of underground activity, kept alive by one intense, avid hope, one idea — that when the revolution finally came, so long awaited and so long desired, there was 'nowhere to go'?

I am sure that when a proper period of time has elapsed, and it will be the turn of the 'February Revolution' to become 'history', there will be found both eye witnesses and participants who will testify to the longsightedness of certain committees, and to goings-on at certain conferences and meetings; and historians will replace, in the time-honoured way, the waves of workers and the soldier mobs with the figures of certain specific 'heroes'. It has happened before and it will happen again. Even following a fresh trail the truth proved very difficult to establish. Immediately after the revolution took place, the 'Officers' Union of 27 February' attempted to trace the train of events by asking for names of participants among the regiments. We received, in answer to the question who brought the Volhyn' Regiment over to our side, seven declarations by seven persons, each one attributing to himself the action which began the February Revolution. We read through seven descriptions of the mutiny which had almost nothing in common with one another. As chairman of the Union, I felt duty bound to get to the truth of the matter, to sort out the question of the seven eye-witness accounts. Finally, I came to an impasse, certain of one thing only — that the regiment most definitely had been led out by an eighth, nameless person, who, as might have been expected, did not send us his account of the matter. And this was during the days when the revolt was alive and breathing before our very eyes, in all its myriad details, when every word could be checked. God knows what will be written when many years have passed, and the graves of the February dead are long overgrown and forgotten.

The truth of the matter was that outside of small factions stewing in their own conspiratorial juices or, even worse, in militaristic and patriotic ecstasies, the socialist parties of those days were completely bankrupt. And so indeed, there was no place to go . . . should I have gone out on the street to join the ranks of the 'eye witnesses'? No — home. I went home. They would be more likely to find me at home.

The Suvorov drill field served as a breakwater. 'Advancing enemy troops' — a few soldiers carrying rifles, without cartridge pouches (even without the belts to hold them), in unbuttoned overcoats — had made it only as far as the guard house halfway between the riding school and the main building of the Academy. No one had entered the building itself. Both the professors and the students had gone home, leaving their swords, for safekeeping, in the Academy museum: they had heard that officers were being disarmed on the streets.

The shooting from Parade Street and Kirochnaya had stopped; three hours had passed since the last shot was heard. As before the Suvorov field was empty and quiet, and as before, on the corner of the Prospect, outside the bank (where, stubborn rumour has it, Kerensky himself attended a revolutionary meeting that very night) the frozen Preobrazhensky guard was still on duty, according to rotation.

By one o'clock in the afternoon, snaking along the sidewalks, seeping in from Nevsky and Basseinaya, crowds of pedestrians began converging on this same spot. Groups formed at the gates and the entrance. They seemed to be anxiously awaiting something. At last, I caught a glimpse of the first soldiers' greatcoats.

The soldiers did not march in step, many did not have any weapons, and they shuffled along the side of the street as if embarrassed by the curious glances of the pedestrians, who were stopping and turning to stare at them . . . . The guard was changing. On schedule. The soldiers pulled themselves together, and got into formation. The commanding officer gave an order. But at that very moment the suddenly numerous mob, which appeared from God knows where, began to crowd around the men, hiding them from view. When, at last, the mob scattered, the guard unit had disappeared: two 'liberated' soldiers, waving their caps, were leading away a young lance corporal with a St. George's Cross upon his chest. The dispersing crowd held surrendered rifles aloft like trophies of victory. The street had been awaiting this. Up it rose, tumultuous with hundreds of stamping feet and piercing whistles. Swarms of adolescents swirled out of the alleys, shouting and firing pistols into the air. A dispirited-looking hackney carriage was seized, in which sat two passengers, an army surgeon and a civilian. The shouts rose to a crescendo. The surgeon stood up in the carriage, with difficulty he frees his meagre sabre from between the folds of his coat, and hands it over to the crowd, and laughingly shouts something back at them. The crowd responds with a joyful roar, parts, and the carriage trots on.

The sound of an automobile horn, brazen and piercing, hits our tense nerves. An impromptu political meeting which has been in full swing on the tram lines in the middle of the street scatters instantly. Again the windows shudder at the sound of hundreds of voices raised in a victorious roar. Making a sharp turn beneath our window as it leaves Suvorovsky and enters Tauride Prospect, a dark blue limousine marked with Imperial gold eagles on the doors glides by, a red flag flapping madly in front and filled to overflowing with armed men. The sailors from the Imperial yacht. They're shouting and waving . . . behind the first limousine a second soon follows, equally elegant and terrifying.

And in the opposite direction, from Tauride Prospect crawls a truck so massive and awe-inspiring that its gears can barely shift. It bristles with bayonets, and overflows with soldiers, workers, students and women. Those in front loom over the drivers, holding weapons cocked and ready to fire.

The Suvorov Prospect is black with people. A political meeting is being conducted in the Zaiats Alley, diagonally opposite the Academy. A dray cart has been unhitched, and orator follows orator on to this shaky platform, which towers above the crowd. Visored caps follow fur hats, which follow bowlers . . . . About three dozen women shuffle by; they are wearing prison gowns and their slippers scuff through the snow. On Suvorovsky they say their good-byes and scatter . . . . Still hatless and without their overcoats, the Preobrazhensky soldiers whom we had hidden are stealthily leaving our gates and mingling with the crowd on the Prospect.

My wife returns from the centre of town: the same thing there. Everywhere there are automobiles and crowds. The arsenal has been taken. They say that about twenty thousand automatic pistols alone have been handed out. There is a lot of firing in the streets, but it all seems to be for show; mostly it's the adolescents who are doing the shooting, almost all of them have revolvers . . . . 'Did you see the women? The criminals from the Litovsky Prison? The jails have been opened.'

The corner continues to be a bubbling cauldron of activity: a boy hidden behind a cornice whistles sharply, with all his might. All at once, everyone turns towards Tauride Street. The crowd surges towards the pavement — a mad crush follows. Pushing their way forward through the retreating crowd, rifle safeties clicking, come armed students and workers. They fan out in a chain across Tauride Street. Once again someone shouts out and waves. And, once more, the crowd reacts, surging forward in answer to the shout. Rifle barrels are lowered. An artilleryman, mounted on a magnificent, deep-chested Caucasian stallion, rides up to the human chain and salutes it with his officer's sabre. 'Hurrah!' Everyone crowds around horse and rider. Street urchins escort him through the crowd, holding on to his stirrups. Caps are thrown into the air. The youths on the pavement madly fire their pistols into the air. Slowly, with a dancing step, the soldier rides by, showing off, making the horse arch its neck by sawing on the iron bit . . . . The Guards Artillery must have mutinied . . . .

Dusk has fallen. The street has grown quieter. Tauride Prospect is blocked with people making their way to the palace.

The telephone in my study rings out.
'Comrade Mstislavsky? Kapelinsky here.'
Kapelinsky was a Menshevik-Internationalist. He had been

Secretary of the Petrograd Association of Workers' Co-operatives during the war years, when I was their Chairman of the Board. Two months ago he had been arrested, as a result of his connection with the now dissolved workers' group of the Military-Industrial Committee, whose leaders — Bogdanov, Gvozdev, and Broido — were the most active members of both the Board and the Association.

If he is at liberty then the Kresty Prison must have been taken.

'Well, we've lived to see the day. Come at once to the Tauride Palace, Room No. 13. But do hurry.'

'I'll be right there.'

I hang up and make preparations to leave, putting on a civilian coat over my uniform so that on the street there will be no misunderstandings concerning my epaulets.

Again the phone rings.

'It's me again, Kapelinsky. Perhaps you'd like us to send a car for you? We're men of influence now . . . .'

'It's really not worth the trouble. I'm two steps away.'

The Tauride Palace — seat of the Duma parliament — seems strangely squat, set too close to the ground. Though every window is lit up there is something ominous in the glow of its glass dome against the dim night sky. In front of the palace, in the courtyard and on the street, bonfires crackle. Trucks, automobiles, crowds of soldiers and civilians; a sea of heads on all sides, everywhere. To right and left, from behind houses and chimneys tightly packed around the palace, crimson pyres are snaking up into the sky. The district court is burning, the gendarme station on Tverskaya, and a fire tower on old Nevsky.

The perimeter and especially the entrance to the palace drive are heavily guarded. To gain entrance one needs a special order, or a pass from a factory committee or military unit. But, in the crush, a few 'ticketless' individuals get through — and I am among them.

'Room 13. To your right and down the corridor.'

I turn right and run into Sokolov — 'Nikolai-Dimitrievich', as he is known to all of political Petrograd. As a lawyer he had made his career defending revolutionaries, and was forever organizing public meetings. He grabs my arm. 'Quick, come with me. The delegates from the regiments who've joined the rising are here. We must organize, we must act. Some units are still loyal to the government. There's fighting in the city.'

The delegates (one is a lance corporal, another is a sergeant major, all the rest are enlisted men) are maintaining their dignity, sitting in a row along the wall. They are unarmed. Sokolov asks what we need to set up a headquarters for our military forces. In the first place, a map of Petrograd.

'Where will we find one?'

'Take it out of Suvorinsky's *All Petersburg*: there must be a copy of the book somewhere in the palace.'

Sokolov rushes away (he was always spry: today he seems veritably winged) to look for a map. We start out by questioning each other, in order to clarify the situation.

Things look not especially promising, from our point of view. It could not be denied that in terms of numbers a definite majority had taken the Revolution's side. The military neighbourhoods adjoining the palace had risen as one — though we had no information concerning the 9th Reserve Cavalry regiment. About fifteen cavalrymen from the regiment are here, in the courtyard of the palace, but as to the whole regiment, it's not clear what happened. Besides the Volhyn' and the Lithuanian regiments, the crews of the Imperial yachts were ours, as well as the chausseurs, the Pavlovsk, the Leib-Grenadiers, the Moscow regiment, the Preobrazhensky battalion (the one stationed on Kiroch-naya Street, nothing had been heard about the one stationed on Millionnaya), the field engineers, and the Guards Artillery. Only the cadet corps of most of the above regiments have remained in their barracks, and are even firing back when 'liberated' soldiers attempt to gain entry. The Finnish regiment hasn't come over; according to certain reports they are holding Tuchkov Bridge, part of Vasilievsky Island and the Petrograd side. The cavalry troops and the Cossacks are either neutral and remain in their barracks, or they have gone over to the commander of the government troops, General Khabalov. The Peter and Paul Fortress remains silent, but it has not declared its allegiance to us; artillery pieces have been placed on its walls and aimed at the bridge, though they have not opened fire yet. The sailors on Kriukov Canal are in their barracks; they have been locked in, and their barracks cordoned off, so it hardly seems possible that they have any idea of what is going on in the city. We do not have the military academies, nor the infantry divisions quartered in the suburbs, and our people's militia may have thrown down its weapons by now.

How many troops Khabalov has, which particular divisions, and where, no one knows exactly. Some troops are standing in formation on Senate Square: infantry, perhaps two squadrons of cavalry, one battery. Apparently they're not 'ours', since we do not have a single company in formation. On Palace Square there are also troops; that seems to be the main headquarters of Khabalov's forces. The Naval Academy is with him, but the telephone exchange apparently remains neutral: it is servicing calls from the Tauride Palace. But perhaps this is done with a hidden purpose in mind, in order to gain information. They themselves can send messages using the military telegraph.

The railway stations remain a mystery.

Analyzed in conventional military terms, our situation would seem quite catastrophic. Of course, Khabalov had already made an elementary mistake: by pulling his troops into the very centre of the city he allowed the revolt to engulf him on all sides. He should have broken out with all possible speed, out of the 'quarantined' zone and beyond the city limits, where he could attract reinforcements. Having isolated Petrograd, the 'hotbed' of revolt, he should have begun a planned, concentric advance. This strategy, in past revolts, and especially in 1905-7, invariably and swiftly left the government forces victorious. In the city itself, the very atmosphere is revolutionary, and this leads to the deterioration of morale much more surely than any barricades . . . . We, for our part, placed all our hopes on this atmosphere, one might say on this 'elemental force'. On it alone.

But . . . was there a truly revolutionary atmosphere in the city? I thought back to that morning's meeting of the Preobrazhensky regiment, recalled the crowds of disarmed soldiers wandering around the city, the boys firing their pistols into the air, and the automobiles rushing up and down the streets. If only we had one, only one division which remained in close-knit formation. We had neither artillery, nor machine guns; neither commanding officers, nor field communications. First Lieutenant Filippovskii, an old comrade from the SR military organization of the 1900s, who had come fifteen minutes after I arrived, was the only other commissioned officer in the palace. A certain captain from an infantry division had wandered in, listened to our staff report, then wandered out again, shaking his head and saying, 'A fellow could get into trouble around here. Just as much chance as a snowball in hell.'

Khabalov's daylight attempt to move some divisions over to our 'fortress city' against the Volhynians failed because the crowds had put a stop to all traffic; his officers could not take it upon themselves to use armed force. But when night falls, the crowds will disperse, and there will no longer be a living, if unarmed, barricade of revolutionary workers between us and Khabalov. It will be army against army then, and who is to say if ours will be the stronger side?

Tonight the government forces must attack. If there is anyone there with any sense this is obvious. Of course Khabalov resembles Gallife, who suppressed revolutionary Paris in 1871, only in the cut of his pants, and has no great talents as a strategist: but in his staff might there not be found a 'corporal with a head on his shoulders'? And if that is so, how should we meet the enemy?

The palace was overflowing with soldiers. All of them were tired and hungry, and their deputies themselves refused to try and organize these men into military formation. They realized that it was 'public enthusiasm' alone which still held them up.

To take them away from the 'public and the people', to move them out into the terrifying gloom of the streets, into the darkness of the empty and frozen railway stations, to send them out on reconnaissance or guard duty — it seemed wiser not to attempt it.

'Why put either ourselves or them through all this trouble?' say the deputies, shaking their heads. 'Today has worn the soldiers out. And another thing — many of them aren't used to serving without an oath of allegiance; it's rather like travelling light, without any luggage.'

The deputies themselves are increasingly drawn to the 'Soviet of Workers and Soldiers Deputies', about to open its session in the adjoining auditorium, and away from General Staff Headquarters. Some of them even say as much: 'We haven't come to you, we're on our way to the Soviet.' It's that very same attraction, towards 'the public and the people'. Besides, they've clearly had enough, they don't want to hear any more military slogans. They've come to hear something else.

Well, perhaps they're right . . . .

And yet, we really ought to hit Khabalov before he hits us.

Our room is slowly filling up with people who have come to hear the Soviet. The adjoining room is packed to capacity. There are many workers, but also the intelligentsia of various shades across the Left spectrum, and ordinary correspondents. The Labour Faction of the Duma is there to a man: it is to them that the Chair belongs, they are our hosts — along with the Social Democrat deputies to the Duma, Skobelev and Chkheidze. From the radical Left I see only the Bolshevik

Shlyapnikov, the Socialist Revolutionary Alesandrovich, and two or three fellow-conspirators from our 'underground days' of 1906 and after.

Sokolov, who seems to have taken charge, hurries from group to group. The flapping folds of his frock-coat seem particularly inappropriate at such a tense moment. (Incidentally, he did bring us a map of the city, apparently from the office of the Duma's Chairman, Rodzianko.)

We have been asked to move; Rooms 41 and 42 are now assigned to the General Staff Headquarters of the uprising. They are located in the opposite wing of the palace — the office of the Vice-Chairman of the Duma, Nekrasov, and the hall adjoining it. Both information and people will be directed there, especially any officers — if they should appear.

The deputies from the troops have already disappeared in the crowd which is awaiting the opening of the Soviet; and so I go to Nekrasov's office alone.

A spacious empty room. The chandelier is blazing away. At the desk, beneath a lamp which is also lit, sits Kerensky. He is wearing a frock-coat, his tie is askew, and he is signing papers which are handed to him by someone whom I do not recognize, who wears a Russian shirt beneath his jacket. Carefully, but with a flourish, he stamps them with an official seal.

We shook hands and I sat down opposite him in an empty chair. The man in the Russian shirt took the last paper and left.

'Well now, Sergei Dimitrievich, it seems we have lived to see the day!' Quickly and happily he jumped up and stretched, as if to restore circulation to limbs gone numb. Suddenly, he laughed out loud, slapped his pocket with boyish playfulness, and took from it a huge and ancient door key.

'That's where I have him. That's where I have Shturmer. Oh, if only you could have seen their mugs when I locked him up!'

Another pile of passes was brought in to be signed. Kerensky signed them without looking, scribbling his expansive signature, and continued the story of Shturmer's arrest.

'You should have seen Rodzianko! Why, he had been quite ready to clasp him in a brotherly embrace . . . .'

Then Nekrasov came in. As usual, he was impenetrably good-humoured, slow, rotund, polished and massive. He greeted me with a smile and a few meaningless phrases, then took Kerensky away.

In the next room I heard the buzz of voices. I opened the door and saw Filippovskii, surrounded by about twenty officers from various regiments, mostly second lieutenants and ensigns. Young, happy, excited faces . . . a beginning, at least, seemed assured.

Quickly, we divide the responsibility. Filippovskii takes the Tauride Palace and 'if the worst happens' its defence. This leaves me with everything outside the palace, with the city.

There are no 'local' officers among those who have appeared at the palace; they are all from the front, in Petrograd either on leave or on a mission. Therefore they have no actual ties with the troops in the city. Nevertheless, with their help, a strategy is beginning to emerge. The plan of action is as follows: an officer receives an assignment, then goes to the soldiers who have gathered in the palace, or even to the palace courtyard, and calls for volunteers. It's the Vendée system — as used by the royalist forces during the French Vendée revolt. In this manner it becomes possible to send out companies to guard the Nikolaevskaya and Tsarskoe Selo railway stations, and to reconnoitre the major strategic points in the city. We aren't sending any forces to the more distant railway stations for the time being, since it seems highly unlikely that they would reach their destinations. Then we receive a surprising phone call from the Finland Station. An army surgeon, on his own initiative, has captured the station with a mixed company of soldiers and workers. They have been there for a few hours already. Everything seems quiet, but nevertheless they are asking for reinforcements: such is the power of military tradition.

We have picked out a shock brigade, under the command of a Lieutenant Petrov. I still remember him, an artilleryman with three St. George's Crosses and a gold rifle decoration, brave and strong — it was a pleasure to look at him. He brought a whole company with him to the Tauride — they had been skirmishing with the Pavlovsk Officers School cadets, across the Mars Fields by the Swan Canal, all through the night, even before the Volhynians had risen. The company quickly attracted more men, so that when we got the first alarming news of the enemy's recapture of the arsenal, we sent out Petrov, backed by one hundred and fifty bayonets.

A reinforced reconnaissance troop was sent to the area of the Naval Academy: thirty horsemen, an armed truck, and a company of infantry commanded by an officer from the Caucasus.

In general, the soldiers volunteer much more eagerly than we have anticipated. But they all insist on formal orders, in written form. The Soviet, naturally, has no seals. Therefore, I write the orders on blank sheets which we find in a desk: they are headed, 'Property of the Chairman of the Government Duma'. The seal is big, the paper is heavy and glossy, and all in all the effect is imposing. Our inner organization is also gradually taking shape. One of the rooms in our wing has been turned into a storehouse for weapons, which are being brought to the palace in bushels. Under the supervision of an artillery officer a few girls and student volunteers are sorting the rifles, revolvers, and shells, and preparing the machine gun belts. At present, we have only four machine guns, and these can't be fired. We need to oil them but there is no lubricant. I sent one of the volunteers to the closest apothecary, for some vaseline. The youth disappeared. We waited and waited, sent another one — they both vanished, God knows where. Finally, the first one reappeared, twirling a silver rouble in his hands, in embarrassment.

'Actually it was rather late. All the shops had already shut up for the night.'

There's a revolutionary for you — at a critical moment of the revolt, he stood with a rouble in his hand in front of a locked door, too embarrassed to wake the owner up — and let's not talk about breaking in the door.

'We really should have your portrait done — to hang on the mausoleum of the Russian intelligentsia.'

There was an endless stream of prisoners. At first they brought them one by one; by nightfall droves were being herded in; gendarmes, officers, Third Section men, policemen, and ministers. Like a line of geese up stepped the whole administration of the Petrograd Gendarmerie: at the head a general, at the tail-end the captains, everything according to rank, here just as at their headquarters on Tverskaya Street. Some over-zealous pranksters brought in an extremely ancient, long retired general, who was muttering to himself: he could not understand for the life of him what had happened, and kept on coughing up something about a fire and a pension, until we finally understood the 'joke' and sent him home. A soldier from one of the rebel regiments brought in a policeman's father: 'It's safer here — God knows what could happen in the city now.' And truly, one had to wonder at the degree of self-control practised by the revolutionaries: there were no excesses — even the gendarmes were brought in bandbox fresh, not even their collars had been mussed.

Only once, during that whole night when hundreds of prisoners passed along our corridor, did I catch the scent of blood. A most imposing civilian, with long, well-kept sideburns, was doggedly hanging around the headquarters. At last he was spotted writing something down. This seemed suspicious, and he was brought in for questioning. The search turned up his gun, along with a large sum of money and a work card identifying him as a gendarme colonel of the Third Section — the one dealing with revolutionaries. A Third Section man here — in the very heart of the revolt! The news quickly spread through the palace. I heard the ring of steel on the other side of our closed door, and the angry growl of the ever-growing crowd. Even then, a few words were enough to silence them, and part their ranks to let the prisoner through under escort.

'Gentlemen, this is impossible,' a member of the Duma (his face familiar, though I couldn't recall his name)' reproached us. 'What kind of military headquarters is this anyway, where spies can go as they please? It's against the most elementary rules.'

We look around us. Indeed, the scene does somewhat resemble a bazaar. The moment that the crowd was barred from the palace, and only elected delegates were allowed to enter, the lower halls began to overflow with all 'politically and socially conscious Petrograd', and simply with friends . . . and each of these visitors, down to the very last reporter, felt it was his duty to look us up at General Staff Headquarters and offer advice:

'Why haven't you taken the airfield yet? There must be one somewhere in Petrograd. You know — aeroplanes and all that sort of thing, it's not to be taken lightly.'

'Why haven't you ordered the streets dug up to stop the armoured cars getting through? Khabalov must have a hundred, at least. We heard it today, in the editor's office. It's absolutely certain.'

'Why haven't you blown up the military telegraph yet? It's very simple, you know, just place the dynamite in a stone post, and there you are. In fact, there's exactly such a post very close to the palace.'

'Storm the Peter and Paul Fortress. If you come from the Neva, right up to the gates . . . .'

On second thoughts, it does not seem such a stupid idea to bar the gates. Not against spies, but against good advice.

But there is no need to shut the gates after all. Night has fallen and alarming rumours are spreading up and down the corridors. Supposedly, Khabalov is advancing. Outsiders make haste to depart. On the way out, they stop in one last time . . . to wish us 'the very best' . . . manfully, they clasp your hand. Courageously, they look you straight in the eye. And, straightening their backs, they leave; ever faster, and faster, and faster . . . .

Suddenly there's so much space. Even . . . one might say
. . . too much space.

Exactly at midnight, the inner door to Room 42, the
generally unknown 'insiders' door swung open, and to our
amazement Rodzianko appeared. He was followed by
Colonel Engelgardt, in civilian dress, and another member of
the Duma. One second later, Sokolov and five men from the
Soviet rushed in, from Room 41. Rodzianko — massive and
frowning — was holding a paper in his hands. He was nervous,
which in itself was unusual. He went to the nearest table and
sat down, heavily, with his weight on his elbows. Engelgardt
immediately took the place opposite him. The rest of us, in
response to an imperative nod from Rodzianko, surrounded
their table in a tight ring.

'Gentlemen officers' — the words seemed to be squeezed
out, almost against his will as his eyes slipped disparagingly
over the epaulets of his General Staff, made up mostly of
ensigns and lieutenants — 'the Provisional Committee of the
State Duma has taken it upon itself to restore public order in
the city, which has been shaken by these latest events. You
yourselves must understand that the restoration of order in
the shortest period of time is an absolute necessity as far as
the front is concerned. Colonel Engelgardt of the General
Staff, and member of the Government Duma, is hereby appointed Commandant of Petrograd.'

Engelgardt reddened and with a half-turn bowed his head,
but did not rise from his chair.

Sokolov interrupted sharply. 'The staff has already been
formed, it is already active, we have chosen its members,
there's nothing for Engelgardt to do here. And it must be left
to us alone to decide who will be in charge of whom and what;
the more so since it is not a matter, right now, of maintaining
order, but rather of smashing Khabalov and Protopopov.
Right now we have no need of "appointees" from a "High
Assemblage"; what we do need are revolutionaries. And
furthermore, it is absolutely intolerable that the Petrograd

Soviet, the Soviet of the revolutionary workers and soldiers, the real source of power under the present circumstances, it is intolerable that this Soviet should be kept away from that military staff which it itself has created. The Soviet has already appointed a group of its members to the staff: if the Provisional Committee should care to participate they are welcome, but the majority, the decisive majority, must belong to the Soviet.'

Engelgardt got redder and redder. The officers were upset. Rodzianko, who was frowning in his old disparaging and slightly disappointed fashion, hit the table heavily with the palm of his hand. 'No, gentlemen, since you have mixed us up in this whole affair, be so kind, now, as to give me your fullest attention.'

Sokolov boiled over, and answered with such a phrase that the officers, who had been listening to Rodzianko most respectfully, began to buzz with indignation. They crowded round Sokolov, and everyone began shouting.

Threats were heard. The members of the Soviet also began to shout. In a second, it seemed, fists would fly. We separated the two sides with considerable difficulty. 'You should be ashamed, at such a time. Does it make any difference who "commands"? The main thing is to get the job done . . . what kind of hierarchy do we have here, anyway?'

And to Sokolov we whispered, 'Who cares if it's Engelgardt — it's no skin off our nose. They can name anyone they want, we won't let go of the reins. You will come to an agreement with the Duma, only you can't do it here.' Rodzianko, meanwhile, had freed his bloated body from the armchair and, breathing heavily, was heading for the door. Engelgardt wasn't far behind him. Some of the officers of our staff also hurried away. Indeed, more than half left. For some time we could hear their voices, out in the corridor. Then the voices became more distant . . . not one of them returned to headquarters that night.

'Who is this Engelgardt?' the remaining officers, who had all come from the front, were asking each other. 'Where did he come from?'

I alone knew something of Engelgardt, who had passed through the General Staff Academy during my tenure there. He was an officer from an Uhlan Guards regiment; he owned racehorses, and sometimes took prizes, but never in the steeplechase. He lived with calculated extravagance and had good connections. He only graduated from the Academy thanks to the patronage of the Dowager Empress Maria, for as a student he was very weak. In the State Duma, to which he was elected from the landlords' curia, he was counted with the right-of-centre Octobrists like Rodzianko. And such is his whole 'obituary', a term I use because no matter how many more years he lives, he will never add anything of significance to the above.

We laughed and talked a bit longer, and then went back to our places as though nothing had happened.

Our reconnaissance team did not return, but many volunteers were coming in with news from the different quarters of the city. They all seemed certain of the enemy's growing activity, and assured us that we were clamped in a wide half circle of machine guns, from Staro-Nevsky up Ligovka and almost to the Liteinyi Bridge. Two pieces of news were particularly disquieting. The first came from the Vyborg highway: the bicycle brigade quartered by the railway line, halfway to Udel'na, had fired at the Aivayaz workers when they approached the barracks with a red banner. The workers tried twice to storm the barracks, but each time were thrown back. They had suffered heavy losses and were asking us for help. The second piece of news was from the corner of Ligovka and Chubarov Alley, where a machine-gun nest had been discovered. Soldiers walking along Ligovka tried to capture it with a frontal attack, but the nest held out. An enlisted man who had come from the scene of battle assured us that losses had already reached eighty people, but that the soldiers refused to retreat and were demanding reinforcements. I immediately sent another ensign who had been waiting for an assignment to Catherine Hall to 'raise a cry' and get some

*Plate 4*  Red Guards in the streets of Petrograd

men for the job. While the soldiers were being recruited, I began explaining to the messenger from the beleaguered company how one should attack a fortified building according to the rules of strategy. The soldier listened to me, smiling good-naturedly, and when I had finished he said, 'You're absolutely wrong, your honour. It's just that we mostly have men there who haven't seen fighting: they can't stand up to a machine gun. If we had about thirty fellows from the front we'd have wiped them out, there's nothing to it. As for your surrounding movements and manoeuvres, and other fancy stuff — well, Lord preserve us from all that when cops are concerned. We'll just crack them with our thumbnails and wipe them off, like the lice that they are.'

The night is beginning to take its toll. In fortification points scattered all around the city, nerves are fraying. The telephone rings ceaselessly. Messages multiply. Everywhere they're demanding reinforcements. The more the reports flood in, the more exaggerated and fantastic they become.

The surgeon is calling from the railway station: an enemy column apparently approached the station, then moved on after an exchange of fire. Rumour has it that the infantry is moving in on them. 'Reinforcements, reinforcements!'

A reconnaissance mission (one automobile) has returned from Zagorodnoe: it was shot at from the Tsarskoe Selo Station.

The chausseurs report from their barracks that an un-identified unit, apparently of monarchist persuasion, is attacking them.

They are demanding reinforcements from the Nikolaev-skaya station. Again! We've already sent four companies there . . . and not one of them has reached their destination: all dispersed along the way . . . .

It is becoming harder and harder to form new detachments: people are tired, and have gone to bed. In the courtyard no one remains by the bonfires except the sentries. The tide from the city has stopped: we only get the occasional 'headhunter' now. That's what we call the people who, on their own, are 'hunting' policemen and Third Section employees. From time to time they show up at the palace to hand over the dead men's weapons and warm themselves.

Our rooms are almost empty: all the officers are out on assignment; I have kept back only two lieutenants, in case of an emergency.

The emergency soon appears: a huge crowd is reportedly gathering in front of the government alcohol warehouse, by Tauride Park. If they break in, the revolution will drown in a sea of vodka.

'Send three hundred bayonets to the warehouse at once — mixed companies of workers and soldiers. They will be commanded by the two remaining officers. The order is imperative, to fire at the first attempt to break into the warehouse — to fire without any mercy. If any of our men touch a single bottle, they are to be shot on sight.'

Around four o'clock in the morning the reconnaissance mission to Palace Square returns. They had reached no further than Morskaya: by the telephone exchange they came under machine-gun fire from the cellars. The tyres of the armoured truck were shot out, it was abandoned by its crew, the driver was killed and the infantry scattered. The dragoons alone came back with this report.

People come and go, in an ever changing crowd. They are waiting for orders and assignments. And I write them out, sheet after sheet, numberless sheets, still on those same Duma blanks. And it seems to me that I am scattering these pitiful sheets of paper like rose petals into a raging storm, covered as they are with meaningless signs, absolutely powerless to change anything.

Those who receive the orders do not fulfil them; those who act, act without orders . . . . And, after all, could it have been otherwise, during a revolution?

It's after five now. Our 'front line' has apparently quietened down: there have been no more reports for some time, the telephone rings feebly. There are no signs of a Khabalov offensive; it must be even worse for him than it is for us. I step out for a moment to see what is going on in the palace. The corridors are lined, on either side, with sleeping bodies. Soldiers, soldiers and more soldiers . . . they sleep with their rifles pinned under their arms, lying any old how, as though they had set up camp on a forced march. It is difficult to breathe in Catherine Hall. In the arsenal people are hard at work: shells, rifles and pistols are lying in piles; they have all been counted and are now being entered into a ledger.

Filippovskii has everything under control. Our machine guns have been hoisted on to the palace roof, but it's all for show, since they still don't work. On the street, with their barrels facing the Liteinyi Prospect stand four guns; these are in excellent condition, and they have enough shrapnel and shells to service them.

My throat is dry. They say that there is a mess somewhere, but where?

Across from our quarters are the rooms of the Duma representatives: on the couches, on the chairs, in the armchairs, on the tables, even on the floor, in all sorts of strange poses sleep 'the politicians', both familiar and unfamiliar. Kerensky, his frock-coat spread out about him, sleeps draped over a small couch, bent like a pretzel, with his mouth wide open. He is snoring sweetly.

The phone in Room 41 is ringing again.

Around eleven in the morning, when the awakened palace was buzzing like a disturbed bee-hive, Engelgardt showed up again. This time, he was wearing the uniform of the General Staff. We had not expected the 'commandant' so early. Things must really be bad for Khabalov's loyalist forces.

Actually, from his very first words it became apparent that he had no intention of 'taking over' as yet; we limited the business at hand to mutual exchange of information. The

Duma had access to information that was surprisingly detailed. Almost unconsciously, against my will, an evil thought flashed through my head: instead of sending armed patrols all over town, wouldn't it have been simpler to have asked Rodzianko or Engelgardt to call the Police Department one more time? Engelgardt also informed us in a rather matter of fact tone that Khabalov and his troops, who at first occupied the Admiralty, have now gone over to the Winter Palace. Since Grand Duke Mikhail Nikolaevich* is quartered there, we can hope that he will influence Khabalov to cease resistance, which is hopeless in the present situation. Khabalov only has five regular army and Cossack squadrons under arms, four companies, and two batteries. According to the same Duma sources the Tsarskoe Selo garrison, as well as the units stationed by Strel'na and Oranienbaum, have just come over to our side, so that Khabalov has absolutely no hope of immediate reinforcements.

And if that is the case — then we must end it now. Taking advantage of the presence of two Soviet delegates among the men assigned to our staff we call them out into the next room. It was there that we decided to occupy the Peter and Paul Fortress, in order to avoid having to take the Winter Palace by storm. The threat of bombardment from the fortress should force Khabalov to evacuate the palace, and then, 'out in the open', we should make short shrift of him.

We started gathering a detachment together. Before sending them off I looked into Room 41, where we had left Engelgardt. Everything was in turmoil.

'You may congratulate us,' the 'commander' greets me. 'Captain Myshlaevsky has just telephoned me from the Peter and Paul Fortress. He has temporarily taken over command, after the resignation of its commandant. The fortress has surrendered upon conditions of immunity for its officer staff.'

What rotten luck that Myshlaevsky should have called while we were out of the room!

---

* Probably Mstislavskii confused here the Tsar's uncle Nikolaevich with his brother Aleksandrovich.

Immediately two men were sent out to accept the surrender — one of our artillerymen (Dubois as I recall) and an ensign appointed by the temporary commandant. Our parting words to the ensign were, 'Don't forget the Trubetskoi Bastion.'

'Why, is there a storehouse there?'

'Perhaps you might have heard that under the tsarist regime there was a phenomenon known as "political prisoners"?'

Soon after Myshlaevsky's telephone call a naval officer, in full dress uniform, was brought to us under escort. The commander of a naval crew — No. 18 if memory serves me correctly — he had come as a representative of the naval officers quartered in the Kruikov Barracks 'to clarify the goals and intentions of the revolt, which in turn would serve to define the attitude of the gentlemen officers to the ongoing events'.

Naturally, he directed his inquiries to Engelgardt, who acquainted the captain with how matters stood in a terse but nevertheless ambiguous fashion (apparently our presence embarrassed him). The emphasis was on Rodzianko's slogan, 'A return to order'.

'But what are your political goals?'

'These Petrograd events in no way predetermine the ultimate picture . . . in this sense. The Provisional Committee has not yet put forward any political programme, as is apparent from its published appeals.'

'Yes, of course, for them it's neither "Yes" nor "No". On the other hand, the proclamations coming from the Soviet are much franker. And on the street corners and in the barracks, among the sailors, they're franker still.'

Engelgardt shrugs nervously. 'How can the Provisional Committee be held responsible for idle street rumours? I have already explained the true goals of the Committee, while the declarations of the Government Duma, in my personal view, are in no way ambiguous.'

'Even if all this is true, the gentlemen officers in whose

name I have the honour of speaking would like a formal guarantee that these events are in no way directed against the monarchy as such. Only under such circumstances can the question of our cooperation be broached.'

The longer the captain spoke, the redder Engelgardt got (he had a truly amazing capacity for blushing). As the captain utters his last few words our people are already rising to their feet. With downcast eyes, nervously shuffling papers, Engelgardt is only forestalling the inevitable when he says, 'Your statement .forces me to place you under arrest, Captain, pending a full investigation of your plenipotentiary authority.'

'But Colonel,' protests the prisoner, pushing out his bemedalled chest. . . .

We nodded to the soldiers standing at the door. 'Take this gentleman to police headquarters.'

Engelgardt wrinkles his brow, glances up at the clock . . . and disappears, once again.

The sudden appearance of the 'commandant' was a sure portent of things to come. Khabalov capitulated soon afterwards. He was brought in, along with Mayor Balk and a whole chorus line of police officers of various ranks.

The 'Duma information' was confirmed on all counts. Even Grand Duke Michael's 'influence' had been anticipated correctly; the Grand Duke had simply ordered Khabalov and his staff to vacate the Winter Palace immediately, 'so as not to subject the palace to the danger of an attack'. And since the Navy Ministry had asked the 'defenders of the throne' to vacate the premises of the Admiralty on precisely the same grounds even before they had taken over the Palace, there was nothing left for these generals, having been thrown out on the street, but to try and save their own skins — which they proceeded to do.

Khabalov's soldiers also turned up; all without rifles.

'Well, where are your rifles?'

'As soon as they ordered us to the barracks, in view of the circumstances of both the autocracy and the war having been ended, they told us to hand over both the rifles and the ammunition to the sailors who'd give us a receipt. Or else, as the general said, the bloody things would be taken from us on the streets anyhow.'

The city is ours.

Now the only possible blow can come from the front, from Dvinsk and Pskov. However . . . it hardly seems possible that strategy could have given way completely to politics. It's true that shots still ring out in the streets; the Protopopov police machine gunners are scattered throughout the city. Due to the bad blood between them and the insurgents they can expect no mercy, and thus cannot surrender. Besides, they have been cut off from all communication with their 'headquarters'; as they lug their machine guns from rooftops to attics, they do not have any idea that our side has won and their resistance is futile. In any case, they continue to make their presence felt: here and there, moving from street to street, the dry rattle of a furious but harmless machine-gun fire is aimed at the crowds of demonstrators. It is harmless because the snipers usually choose to set up their guns in the attics of large multi-storied houses, from which they are harder to remove but less likely to hit anyone. To knock out these machine-gun nests is extremely difficult: they lead us a merry chase. Nevertheless, this is no longer a battle, merely the death throes of the police establishment.

·The only serious opponents remaining — the bicycle brigades stationed along the Vyborg highway, surrendered towards morning as soon as they came under fire from the two armoured vehicles sent out against them.

The city is ours — but it remains very much a turbulent sea. As before, our pickets and patrols disappear in the chaos of crowded streets and the unceasing din of wild gunfire. And the tension here at headquarters continues to mount. For it is at this moment, when the mood of the 'first day' is ebbing, that excesses may be expected. On the city's peripheries a few alcohol warehouses have already been broken into. Yet the danger is not over, the revolution has not been secured. From the telegrams intercepted for us by the sailors at the telegraph it is clear that General Staff Headquarters intends to put up a fight: a 'punitive expedition' is being organized. General Ivanov 'Iudich', the infamous 1905 'pacifier of Kronstadt', has already started towards the city at the head of the first troop train. We must prepare to meet him — but how, in the midst of this primeval chaos?

The situation was made even more complex by the fact that a link existed between the 'pacifier' Ivanov and the Provisional Committee (particularly with the 'Commandant of Petrograd', Engelgardt): a direct, even an official link. I learned during the course of a conversation with a General Staff officer whom I happened to meet in a corridor of the Tauride Palace that 'a liaison officer', Colonel Tilli, had been sent out to meet Ivanov's detachment. As if this were not enough, Colonel Domanevsky was also preparing to leave us in order to take up a position as head of Ivanov's staff, again as agreed by the same Provisional Committee. I had known Domanevsky before my time at the Academy, when he was an officer of the First Artillery Guards: here was definitely a man with Black Hundreds leanings. Both the choice of man, and the fact that he had been sent from a 'city in arms' at the request of the commander of a punitive force, were indicative of the realities of our situation. In the words of Iudich, 'a reliable officer' was wanted, someone 'familiar with the situation in the city, to take on the responsibility of heading the General's staff'. Obviously our local 'defenders of law and order' have no intention of putting up any resistance to the 'defenders of law and order' moving from the front. And since this is clearly the situation, we must be doubly vigilant. . . .

We then established contact with the railway workers. They promised not to let any troop trains pass which they suspect of 'punitive intentions'. A telephone call is made to the Tsarskoe Selo garrison. They will be ready to defend the Petrograd road should any attempt be made on the capital itself. They are full of enthusiasm and sincere good wishes: in short, they seem reliable. Here, in Petrograd itself, we have already gathered all available forces. Despite the fact that the troops are gradually returning to their barracks, the state of primeval chaos still prevails, and the complete lack of organization continues unabated . . . . Somehow we manage to shore up the guard at the railway stations and to form a shock detachment, consisting of three infantry battalions and a division of heavy artillery, as a strategic reserve. . . .

Another night passes without sleep, just like the last one — the same tense atmosphere, the same essentially futile attempts to steer the raging, rebellious city into navigable waters. We 'dose' machine-gun nests after chasing them all over the city, we zealously guard the alcohol warehouses: in short, we await Iudich.

In the morning the 180th Infantry Regiment arrived: in full marching order, complete with officers and regimental colours, machine guns and supply wagons. At once everyone breathed easier — at last we had a well-knit, solid, battle-ready unit — in case of any difficulties from the front.

Rail dispatches informed us that besides the Tarutinsky regiment, which had already fraternized with our men at Aleksandrovsk, and the Georgievsk regiment, there were no other troop trains on the rails, outside that of Iudich himself, still pursuing a steady course towards our Tsarskoe Selo checkpoint.

At last we could go home for an hour or two: bathe, have a bite to eat, change our shoes . . . . We had been up and about for almost fifty hours.

Around five o'clock in the afternoon I returned to the Tauride Palace, to Room 41, and could hardly recognize it.

Office desks, obtained from God knows where, were grouped sedately in rows in a strict hierarchy clearly determined from above. A couple of dandyish scribes, and two or three typists, fashionably dressed with curls bunched low over their foreheads and combs stuck into their chignons, were already rattling away at typewriters. Sparkling with aiguilettes and epaulets, smoothly shaven and well-coifed persons (none of whom had been seen during the past two nights) were placing an array of files on various desks. The final touch was provided by the adjutants, in their patent leather boots and tightly fitting breeches, oozing self-confidence, even gaiety, fluttering back and forth between the typists and the administrative desks.

Engelgardt sat entrenched behind 'my' desk. He was surrounded by a whole constellation of officers from the General Staff — of the same Guards colouration as himself. There they were — Prince Toumanov, Samson von Gimmelshtern, the corpulent Iakubovich of the Giorgievskii regiment, Romanovsky, and others . . . .

The discussion centred on a *de facto* restoration of the Petrograd Staff Headquarters — at least until the fate of the 'real' General Staff Headquarters could be determined. The latter had crawled into the woodwork on 27 February, and had still not reemerged into the light of day. This temporary Staff Headquarters was to be known as the 'Army Commission of the Government Duma Provisional Committee'. In the time-honoured fashion of all General Staff Headquarters, responsibilities were already being delegated among its various newly-created branches . . . .

A clammy horror was slowly creeping up to my heart. I stepped out into the hall. There, leaning against the wall, stood one of the comrades who had been with us from the first hours of the revolt; he was in charge of the motorized transport.

'What are you doing here?'

'And have you anything better in mind?' he said with a bitter smile. 'I've been dismissed, and in no uncertain terms.'

'Dismissed?'

'Yes, quite simply dismissed. Stupidly, I rushed home

earlier on today — only for an hour. When I got back I discovered that whole crew' — he nodded towards Room 41 — 'already entrenched. And behind my desk sits a bandbox-fresh little squirt. . . . Devil knows who.'

'In other words, the patent leather boots had taken over,' I laughed.

'That's it precisely. Patent leather. Lying in front of him I see my own order book, and all my other things. I ask him, "May I sit down?" And he replies, "And what, precisely, is your business here?" He even squints, damn his eyes, as he says it. "My business is the following — this is the motorized division, isn't it?" "Yes, it is." "Well, I'm in charge of it. Those are my files which you have in front of you on your desk." "Oh, so these are your files," he says. "Excellent. Allow me to express the sincere appreciation of the Army Commission." And the bastard shoves his hand out at me. Then with a change in tone, "In the future we shall have no further need of your services." '

'And that's the way he put it?'

'Exactly,' said the comrade, digging his fists deeper into the pockets of his worn leather jacket.

'And where are the rest of our boys?'

'God alone knows. Filippovskii and two or three others are in the Soviet. About a dozen stayed, you can see them in there typing away between salutes. The rest, I imagine, were kicked out . . . not their type.'

'You're right about that . . . not their type at all. Comrade, you go along to the Executive Committee. I'll meet you there . . . just want to check on what exactly they're conjuring up with Iudich.'

Back in Room 41 I turned to Engelgardt. The first train of Ivanov's punitive division was already at Vyritsa.

'I hope that you will agree to stay on for one more round of night duty,' Engelgardt asked me. 'As you can see, this is all still new to us.'

I agreed.

The night shift has been moved upstairs, into the new quarters of the 'Army Commission'; apparently, they wanted to make sure that no confusion, even in terms of physical location, could possibly arise between them and the 'Revolutionary Staff Headquarters'. Rooms 41 and 42, despite their present bureaucratized and gentrified appearance, were too strong a reminder of those February nights.

Now I had very little work to do. During my absence my responsibilities had been taken over by Engineer Palchinsky, introduced to me as 'a friend of Army Commission Chairman, Aleksander Ivanovich Guchkov'. In contrast to the new mobilized division chief described above, Palchinsky was nauseatingly polite. He attempted to make me feel, in every possible way, that I had not been removed from my duties, not in the least. In reality, however, I was no longer allowed to send any direct orders to our troops in the field.

A colonel from the General Staff, known to me like the rest of Engelgardt's retinue from my days at the Academy, briefed me as to developments concerning Iudich: 'His Majesty is in Pskov; abdication is expected. A special Duma commission — Guchkov, Shulgin and someone else "in authority" — are already on the way to Pskov.'

The punitive expedition had taken on truly grandiose proportions; thirteen battalions, sixteen squadrons and four batteries for the first blow. However, out of all of these, only the Tarutinskii regiment had actually moved out, and they had come over to our side. Ivanov's Georgievskii battalion was stuck somewhere on the branch lines surrounding Petrograd. Under such circumstances any attempt to take the capital itself was clearly impossible, and Ivanov himself has given up any plans to 'punish the mutineers', and is now solely concerned with reaching the Tsar in the hopes of obtaining further instructions.

Measures have already been taken to forestall even this course of action. Iudich has been told to remain at Vyritsa; God knows how his presence could influence the Tsar. If Ivanov disobeys and attempts to move the Giorgievskii regiment to the Warsaw line over a trunk line, the railway workers have promised to direct his train into a dead-end siding. 'Your "strategic reserve" is located near that trunk line, isn't it?' the colonel enquires.

'And so?'

'And so, we are stewing here for nothing. One officer on duty would have been quite sufficient.'

There is a stir in the neighbouring room. Guchkov has arrived. With him are Polovtsev — calm and elegant as always in a fresh Circassian uniform — and another member of the General Staff.

There had been four of them until Prince Viazemsky was fatally wounded by a stray bullet on Palace Square. Their driver had not heeded the soldiers' orders to stop.

Guchkov is 'very, very happy'. Everything is 'coming along splendidly'. Law and order are 'quickly being restored', and most divisions are 'back in the hands of their officers'. The tone is universally optimistic and self-confident, both among those who arrived with Guchkov, and among the local 'officers on duty'.

Without any embarrassment (for why should my presence embarrass them?) they bandy the word 'comrades' about, enclosing it in disdainful quotation marks. Around me I hear the familiar jargon of regimental meetings and Guards' common rooms.

I am sitting next to Polovtsev on the window sill; we are idly chatting about nothing in particular. Dawn has broken. A cold light illuminates the outlines of the buildings and the lacy domes of the trees in Tauride Park.

Palchinsky is talking in subdued tones to Guchkov. They call me over.

'Aleksander Ivanovich shares absolutely all your views.'

More saccharine. Aleksander Ivanovich gazes at me with disingenuously empty eyes, all the while nodding in perfect rhythm to Palchinsky's drone. Then he asks me point-blank:

'Which position would you like to hold in the Ministry of the Army?'

I did not have to think too long about turning him down.

Guchkov turned away curtly and walked over to the window to talk to Polovtsev. Palchinsky stood around for a bit, attempting with a nervous smile to soften the sharp silence which lay between us.

Through quiet and sleepy halls, past the ballroom where the dim lights flickered off the bayonets of the cadet guards (Rodzianko has already replaced the unreliable 'enlisted men's' watch with cadet guards: the military academies had proved their worth through their neutrality during the February days), past the night watchmen dozing in the empty vestibule, past the quiet corner room where only yesterday machine-gun ribbons crackled under the agile fingers of young girls, I walked into the fresh morning air which, beneath its winter chill, was already hinting, ever so slightly, at the Spring to come. Tauride Street lay empty before me. A strange din was coming from the direction of Kirochnaya Street — a far-off, polyphonous rumbling and screeching. Half-way through Tauride Park (I could already see the Konchansk Dome, from around the corner) a heavy, slow, stream of grey-uniformed bodies was flowing into Tauride Street. The screeching, grinding noise was getting louder. Involuntarily my hand reached down to my holster.

The first soldiers catch up to me. Hundreds of wheels screeching on the icy snow, a regiment of machine gunners approached the Tauride Palace.    They come from Oranienbaum to join: we had been expecting them since yesterday.

I stood there for a long time, watching their silent ranks, exhausted by the long march, file past me. Their machine guns, carefully wrapped in felt, seemed like strange, primeval beasts. And from the noise, from the gleaming copper of machine-gun belts criss-crossed upon their poorly-clad chests, from the pure and silent thought which sprang so clearly from these hundreds of men, and which united them body and spirit into a single whole, a sudden joy came over me. Everything became light and clear again — truly Spring had come.

The dark impressions of the last few hours melted away, and I wanted to shout out loud, in rhythm to the lava stream of machine guns, 'Long live the Revolution!'

*Plate 5* M.V. Rodzianko — last Chairman of the Duma Parliament

# THE SECOND DAY

## The Founding of the Provisional Government

3 March 1917

From early morning on 3 March the crescent-shaped drive of the Tauride Palace was overflowing with demonstrators. The red banners which had replaced the old regimental icons with such ease, the placards lovingly and naïvely executed in red and white paint, the red flags streaming from the bayonets of the Don troops, all formed a background for the bareheaded orators who were shouting at the tops of their voices from the mud-begrimed steps of the palace. Skobelev following Rodzianko, Chkheidze replacing Guchkov . . . .

Rumours from 'reliable sources', 'from Shulgin himself', spread like wildfire through the palace corridors. Their chief subject was the abdication; the Tsar was said to have vacated his throne without a struggle as soon as the army's attitude towards the revolt became clear. Some doubted this scenario; to me, however, and to others who had had the opportunity of closer contact with 'His Majesty', such a turn of events seemed not only reasonable but even psychologically inevitable. It was fully in character with Nicholas's essential trait of not giving a damn for anything in general and the Russian Empire in particular. What would have been strange is if this God-anointed nihilist had fought for the sceptre which had meant no more to him than a walking stick.

As a direct confirmation of this rumour, in the inner rooms of the palace the Provisional Government was already taking shape. When I stopped by the 'Army Commission' rooms, this very process was being discussed there — in whispers, almost on tip-toe, with reverential awe, as if a sacred rite were taking place.

Again a familiar feeling of aversion flooded over me. I was disgusted by the joyous capers of these new members of the almost completely renovated 'revolutionary staff', by the unctuous way in which these colonels respectfully pronounced the names of the 'ministers-to-be'. Again it was becoming unbearable. I felt that below us, in the gilded rooms of the Duma chairman, they were haggling over the distribution of power, haggling like traders at a bazaar, and that these machinations were an insult to the blood which had been spilt in the name of the revolution. I went below to look for my comrades.

'The Provisional Government? Yes, yes, a coalition has definitely been worked out. Kerensky and Chkheidze from the Executive Committee will be included, the former as Minister of Justice, the latter as Minister of Labour.'

'Can this really be true?' I asked myself.

I stop the first familiar face I see, a member of the Executive Committee whom I barely know. 'Is that babbling about a coalition true?'

Perhaps seventy-eight hours without sleep were beginning to take their toll. Was my voice too threatening, did I appear rather on edge? The Executive Committee member, in a calculatedly soothing manner, put his hand on my shoulder.

'Who told you that? It's an outright lie! It's those damned bourgeoises who are spreading this sort of garbage about. There was, of course, a rather serious discussion of the matter. The Duma members wanted some names in the new cabinet which would appeal to the workers and soldiers, and they were particularly adamant about Kerensky. You know, even though Chkheidze is not actually a Jew, from their viewpoint he is not exactly Russian either, so, in other words, they were not too keen on him . . . . Anyway, the Executive Committee categorically rejected a coalition. The proposed government programme did not include two of our basic points: in the first place, the question of immediately proclaiming a democratic republic was bypassed by those gentlemen, though they did refer to some sort of "future constituent assembly"; in the second place, there was no agreement concerning the reorganization of the army. And, in general, the Executive Committee feels that by giving up a modicum of governmental power to Rodzianko, Lvov, and the rest of that company, they are assured of maintaining full freedom for future revolutionary activity.'

I remembered what I had heard at General Headquarters but kept my own counsel. 'So, neither Kerensky nor Chkheidze, right?'

'Right, neither Chkheidze nor Kerensky. That has been officially confirmed.'

And a few minutes later, as I was crossing the Catherine Ballroom, I heard Miliukov (who had already, a little prematurely perhaps, hurried in to congratulate us on this red-letter day for democracy) talking from a podium. Shifting nervously from foot to foot, he was calming the audience's grumblings, which were inspired by his frankly monarchist formulations, by reminding them that his closest colleague in the new cabinet would be Aleksander Fedorovich Kerensky.

Who was fooling whom? Neither side was being honest. The higher ranks of both the Council of Ministers and the Soviet of Workers lied in an equal fashion when they maintained a facade of total intransigence for the benefit of their followers. For the same reason all negotiations and manoeuvres were presented as ruses perpetuated to compel the enemy to make a fatal concession. In reality, however, not only did they have no intention of capsizing one another, but they frantically grasped at any and all grounds for agreement. And this was both inevitable and natural, for despite all the apparent differences in 'name, dialect and social origin', and even in so-called political principles, the members of the Provisional Committee and the Executive Committee, in the overwhelming majority of cases, were united from the first hours of the revolution by one single characteristic which determined all else: this was their fear of the masses.

Oh, how they feared the masses! As I watched our 'socialists' speaking to the crowds which flooded the assembly halls of the Tauride Palace with a red tide of banners, buttonholes and cockades, I could feel their nauseating fear reflected in the depths of my own soul. I felt the inner trembling, and the effort of will it took not to lower their gaze before the trusting, wide-open eyes of the workers and soldiers crowded around them. These eyes were clear, full of anticipation, almost child-like. And yet there was something truly frightening about a General Staff Headquarters manned by such 'children'. They were primordial, almost elemental; and the tattoo of their drums, which scattered the burghers peeking in at the palace windows, hardly spoke of the nursery. Their long years at the front, under the horrifying conditions of the tsarist regime, had served to hone to a razor sharpness those very characteristics which in ancient times caused the elegant pens of the Byzantine chroniclers to tremble when describing the raids of the Rus .... The way they carried their rifles was telling enough — guns trembled with the pressure of the cartridges crammed into the barrel.

As recently as yesterday it had been relatively easy to be 'representatives and leaders' of these working masses; peaceable parliamentary socialists could still utter the most bloodcurdling words 'in the name of the proletariat' without even blinking. It became a different story, however, when this theoretical proletariat suddenly appeared here, in the full power of exhausted flesh and mutinous blood. And when the truly elemental nature of this force, so capable of either creation or destruction, became tangible to even the most insensitive observer — then, almost involuntarily, the pale lips of the 'leaders' began to utter words of peace and compromise, in place of yesterday's harangues. They were scared . . . and who could blame them? There was no ambiguity whatsoever in the attitude of the mass of rebelling workers and soldiers towards the princes, landowners and factory magnates. The very mention of Prince Lvov's chairmanship of the new cabinet raised the hackles of the soldiers' section of our Soviet: 'You mean all we did was exchange a tsar for a prince, and that's it? That wasn't exactly worth fighting for, you know.' Others laughed. 'Well, brothers, here's another joke that's on us. "Tsar" at least has something grand about it — more fitting — and "Emperor" is even better. The word itself has a ring to it, a sound like a trumpet call. But "prince" just isn't the same thing —just doesn't have the same sweep.'

But it was Comrade Savatii, a grenadier who had been awarded the St. George's Cross for valour three times, one of the few to be both 'bemedalled' and elected to serve in the Soldiers' Soviet, who summarized these unofficial discussions with one pithy phrase: 'If they ram him down our throats we'll chew him up and spit him out.'

The Executive Committee was fully aware of these sentiments, of course, and only agreed to the coalition because they felt capable of maintaining control over the masses, whose leaders they had so unexpectedly become. And yet, in order to maintain this control, they first needed to take over the reins of government; and they feared government no less than they feared the workers and soldiers. Not only did they not have any idea what shape the future 'government' would take, but they were not very well acquainted with the workings of its previous forms either. They would be hard put to know exactly what they were fighting for, in the event of a final break with the bourgeois elements in the Duma cabinet.

Under these conditions they naturally could not commit themselves to 'taking power'. And, consequently, they had to make as many concessions as were necessary, within the limits tolerated by the masses, to the KD, Octobrists and others whom they continued to see as masters of the art of government, technicians who possessed the secret of the governing mechanism which somehow continued to elude the Duma socialists. The opposite situation prevailed among the bourgeois element of the Duma. They had no fear of government — on the contrary, they waved their tentacles longingly above the power which lay so temptingly in their path. They knew the byways of government, and certainly had no need of the socialists to guide them. The bourgeoises would never have deigned to associate with these 'people of a certain sort' (the words of the blue-blooded Rodzianko, which were followed by a fastidious shrug, in reference to Chkheidze and Skobelev), had it not been for . . . that same fear of the masses, that terror before unchained primordial forces. Miliukov and the others, no less than the Executive Committee, knew the people's mood. Under these circumstances, the socialists were the lightning conductor they needed. Thus, from two different positions both sides came to the same conclusion: that in order to survive, they had to stick together, since neither had any grassroots support.

And since it was equally impossible to admit this situation either to themselves or to the masses at large, both sides lied, to their own supporters and to each other. The two political groupings assured each other of their undying devotion — an obvious lie; they lied to their followers by presenting their fraternal embrace with 'the enemy' as actually being a death grip. Were some of them lying unconsciously? Perhaps. Fear is commonly held to cloud reason . . . .

The view from the sidelines, however, was mercilessly clear.

At dusk, walking along the lower corridor on the right-hand side of the palace, I met Kerensky. We exchanged a few empty phrases, and I was already holding out my hand for a farewell handshake when he suddenly pulled me off to one side, all the way to the wall, and began to whisper rapidly in my ear.

'I have been offered a post in Lvov's cabinet as Minister of Justice. I would be the only socialist. What's your opinion: should I or shouldn't I?'

I shrugged. 'How can one either take or offer advice when making decisions of this sort?'

A twitch passed through Kerensky's whole body, and he straightened up. 'So even you don't know?' he asked sharply, through clenched teeth, with a special emphasis on the 'you'. Turning, he entered the 'Provisional Government' office, and slammed the door.

We met again half an hour later, at a session of the Soviet during which the Executive Committee was to announce its decision concerning the 'transfer of power' to the Lvov cabinet. This cabinet did not include a single socialist member, since the Executive Committee categorically denied Kerensky's request for permission to accept the Justice portfolio.

The Executive Committee was faced by a truly difficult problem. They had to convince the representatives of the revolutionary masses to agree to the transfer of government into the hands of the bourgeoisie — despite the fact that no bourgeois elements had participated in the actual revolt. At first glance this seemed to be psychologically impossible. To force their class enemies to take over the wheel of the ship of state, with a pistol pressed to their temple, to make them guide this ship wherever the workers and soldiers wanted it to go, because the latter still did not understand the mechanics of government: how was it possible to convince anyone of the honesty and good faith of such a metaphor?

And yet this was precisely what the leaders of the Executive Committee managed to do. They mobilized all their powers of persuasion, and unleashed a veritable deluge of revolutionary rhetoric. The stakes were very high, of course: for them it was literally 'to be or not to be', and this made their appeals that much more powerful and sincere. A special pathos reverberated through their speeches — did it matter that it was inspired by fear? Fear gave a special drama and colour to their words and made them that much more gripping. To their untrained and naïve audience, so unused to freedom of speech, their words were indeed spell-binding.

The auditorium, overcrowded yet paradoxically exuding the very air of freedom, reacted to the orators with an answering tremor. And ever so slowly the gazes of the soldiers and workers began to soften at the sight of this strange 'mass' which was being celebrated before them in the name of freedom. Savatii was not alone in experiencing tears of joy slowly rising in his throat. The spirit of reconciliation, of an almost pascal peace, wafted over the hall . . . .

It was at this moment that Kerensky took the podium.

His special characteristic as an orator had been, from way back, an extreme sensitivity to the mood of his audience. He did not control his listeners, it was rather the listeners who controlled him. Because of this he was absolutely helpless in a hostile environment: he hadn't the strength or will power to alter the feelings or the thoughts of the masses. When addressing an indifferent crowd he was invariably colourless. But he was passionate, even brilliant, when he rhetorically rode in on the waves of an enthusiasm which was already present, skilfully keeping on the crest of the crowd's passions. And that evening he could not help but speak smoothly, freely and powerfully, opening up his own soul to match the openness which he saw in the shining eyes of the workers' and soldiers' deputies, crowding before him.

And so his speech in his own defence rang out with a special, unusual force.

His doubts occasionally surfaced, breaking through the rhythmic cadences of his rolling words. And at that moment they truly pained him, because the universal feeling of lofty idealism which permeated that auditorium had a hypnotic effect on Kerensky, and under its influence he was sincere and honest, even with himself, and he began peering into certain nooks and crannies of his conscience which had been closed to him the day before, and which doubtlessly would be shut tight

*Plate 6* Aleksander Fedorovich Kerensky — last chairman of the Provisional Government

again tomorrow, closed with the first wave of his ministerial seal — closed tight, for a long time.

His speech was a passionate plea for moral support, for justification — from its first sharply honed presentation of the question of confidence, to its closing sentences, when success was already assured, and the words themselves began to waver, along with the orator, as if from exhaustion. And it was only in these final phrases that he made a fatal *faux pas*:

'As Minister of Justice, I had the representatives of the old regime in my power, and I decided not to let them out of my hands . . . . My first step was to free the representatives of the social democratic faction . . . .'

Nothing reveals the all-forgiving and conciliatory mood of his audience more clearly than the fact that they even forgave him this shamefully self-serving phrase. For me it completely overrode, in the span of one heart-beat, the whole of the passionate confession which came before.

Even this the crowd accepted. They forgave. His final shriek was drowned by the din of the applause. And he felt this to be his justification. By the same token, of course, the new cabinet was also approved. The Executive Committee quickly called for the voting to begin. Chkheidze turned his smiling gaze towards Skobelev, good-humoured and drowsy-looking, as usual; they had won the skirmish.

Actually, only a mere handful remained irreconcilable and uncompromising, totally opposed to any agreement at all with the bourgeoisie. But they expressed themselves bookishly, without a spark of life, throwing about words of wisdom which fell like lead weights in the midst of the excited audience. The results were a foregone conclusion. The more sensitive opponents of the compromise abstained altogether: it hardly seemed proper to voice one's doubts during a matins service, and it would have been worse than useless to try and reverse the tide of popular enthusiasm, merely serving to cast a pall over this joyous occasion, for many the first such occasion in their lives.

The 'new government programme', which was a summary

of the agreement with the Duma representatives, as presented by the Executive Committee, was accepted by an overwhelming majority. The suspicions which had been lulled by this session found their sole expression in two points, which were included as amendments to the original document: first, the demand that the Provisional Government guarantee the immediate implementation of all the points on the agenda, despite the continuation of the state of war; second, the creation of what was essentially a 'watchdog' committee, made up of representatives from the Executive Committee of the Soviet of Workers' and Soldiers' Delegates to monitor the activities of the government — 'the pistol at the temple', so to speak. Kerensky could have chosen to regard this measure as a vote of 'no confidence'; his own presence in the cabinet was clearly felt to be an inadequate guarantee. But he was not offended. Besides, he had already left the hall.

The mood created during the Soviet session was still holding firm when the deputies, having finally approved the resolution, rushed back into the Catherine Ballroom, to the waiting masses. That evening the Tauride Palace was just as crowded as on the first day of the revolt. This made the contrast between 'then' and 'now' all that much more apparent. And, shall I confess it — I missed the old watchfulness of the halls and ballrooms, the frightened eyes of the 'politicians', inching their way along the sides of the corridors, and I missed the old crowds, armed to the teeth, boldly rolling through the Palace, illuminated by the sharp light of life or death. Of course 'then' the night had been lit up by the fires in the city, 'now' it was lit up by the holiday atmosphere itself. But I could not chase away the unwanted thought that these people, happily crowded together, shoulder to shoulder, were not actually celebrating freedom as such, they were joyously heralding the return of normalcy, and the fact that the dark cloud of unknowing, which had been hanging over the city for the last few days, had now been lifted. Once again the old familiar landmarks of ordinary, day-to-day life had reappeared. Therefore it was not at all surprising to see, now high above the crowds, those very same 'heroes' who only yesterday were making their way stealthily along corridor walls. With chests thrown back they rained phrases brilliant as fireworks down on our heads: 'Liberty, liberty, liberty!' The very air beneath the palace dome reverberated with this word, in a never-ending carillon of ringing variations — this word, which only yesterday seemed so far away, so unattainable, and which now was being bandied about by one and all.

And, dare I confess it, I envied all of them to the point of pain — all those happy people with shining crystal-clear gazes, who so sincerely believed that it was all over. That the revolution had been carried out, that soon the last, misguided shots would die out in the last God-forsaken alley-ways, and life would once again begin to flow according to its familiar tempo, only with the added benefits which would be reaped from our February deeds. . . . I, however, could not rid myself of the painful awareness that this wasn't so, that a long, hard road still lay before us, a tangle of pitfalls and contradictions which would not be as easily severed, with one blow, as the first knot had been by our revolt of 27 February.

As I was listening, with closed eyes, to another in a succession of orators, shaggy and ecstatic, barking the same sounds over and over again about Liberty from the podium — suddenly the clear, quiet and hard words of my wife came to my mind: 'Over? Oh no — it can't be over. Not enough blood has been shed.'

If only we could share their faith . . . . But we don't believe, we know. . . ! And, allow me to repeat myself, this alienation from the mood of universal exaltation was extremely painful for me.

On the podium, in the depths of the Catherine Ballroom, by the entrance to the meeting rooms of the Government Duma, orator followed orator. And the crowd applauded them all.

Each and every one. Even Miliukov. . . .

The sight of his figure brought a smile to my face; he was so very festive, so obscenely happy, he so obviously felt himself to be 'king of the mountain'. Well, what can one say . . . the ministerial portfolio hadn't exactly come easily to the old man. How many times, at various stages of his career, had I bumped into him during his long haul to the rank of minister. I remember the apartment on Nizhegorodskaya where in the Autumn of 1905 he, the delegate of the 'Liberation Union', quizzed me, the Vice-Chairman of the All Russia Officers Union and a member of the Socialist Revolutionary military organization, concerning the possibility of an armed uprising. I remembered his role of prompter during the 'first conference of the *zemstvos* and the municipal delegates' — he was just as much an unofficial observer there as I was myself, just as illegal, hiding out with me in the same cubby hole. His election to the Government Duma provided him with an aura of solid stability and gave his words a certain weightiness. Then came the stint as the 'silent partner' in the foreign ministry. And now, finally, the highest step has been reached, the zenith of all desires, the culminating point of a twenty-year journey. Culminating indeed. For it was clear that the fate of all such ministers, railroaded into their posts by the revolution, was sealed.

As soon as the typically Georgian cadences of Chkheidze rang out, the audience pricked up its ears. And so did I. Everyone knew that during this speech, directly or indirectly, the price of the Duma representatives' agreement to a coalition government would have to be revealed. He began, as did the majority of the speakers, with a call for 'unity among all revolutionary forces', and he worked this theme for quite a while. It even seemed that he would not touch on the crux of the matter at all. But towards the end of his speech one could see that he was gathering his forces. Finally, he frowned, lowering his brows together in a grimace peculiar to Georgians when they wish to be particularly frightening. And he made an acute and passionate appeal against certain 'provocative pamphlets, of apparently socialist democratic origins, which were being handed about the barracks, and which were inciting the soldiers against their officers'. I laughed to myself — there it was — of course, support of the military was the price.

After Chkheidze came many others. Dear, joyous Kapelinsky, Secretary of the Executive Committee, and even Stepan Ivanovich, a Menshevik from *The Day*, a dried-out old journalist . . . .

In short, we had come to the end of a very long day.

Last but certainly not least, just before the curtain came down, Kerensky appeared. He did not mount the platform in the middle of the hall from which everyone else addressed the crowd, but spoke from the left-hand balcony. Dressed completely in black, pale and exultant, thin as a candle, it was difficult to recognize in this bloodless and powerful apparition that same 'man on the edge', shifting this way and that, with whom I had spoken just a couple of hours before in the corridor. He fixed his strangely empty and lacklustre gaze above the crowd, somewhere into the distance. And somehow even his voice sounded different; the clipped words of old were at odds with his new, turgid way of speaking. In fact, the whole figure of Kerensky, from head to toe, seemed somehow contrived and false.

An unkind thought flashed through my tired brain, only to be dismissed immediately, as being too dishonourable.

'I am citizen Kerensky, the Minister of Justice . . . .' As the clipped sound of his clear-cut syllables rolled on, his familiar voice suddenly seemed quite strange. The ballroom veritably rocked, from edge to edge, with cries of approval and applause.

'I hereby announce that the Provisional Government has embarked upon the fulfilment of its responsibilities, with the support and approval of the Soviet of Workers' and Soldiers' Delegates.'

He placed a pale hand upon the satin lapel of his frock-coat and pulled out a blood-red handkerchief with which he fanned his face.

As though on cue, the crowd responded with a new storm of applause. Its roar drowned out the sole dissenting voice, desperately shouting something which is completely inaudible, yet which is understood by all . . . .

This called forth an even more desperate round of applause, as joyously excited voices shielded and supported one another — one must have faith, one must believe. The feeling is that of a pascal liturgy.

'The New Resurrection, the Holy Resurrection. . . .'

But they all understood. Even Kerensky. He flushed and answered the challenge in turn.

'The agreement which has been reached between the Committee of the Government Duma and the Executive Committee of the Soviet of Workers' and Soldiers' Delegates has been approved by the Soviet Deputies by a vote of several hundred to fifteen.'

And, once again, the red handkerchief unfurls like a flag, and once again it is followed by a mad flurry of clapping.

After a pause, Kerensky continued.

'The first act of the new government will be the immediate publication of a full amnesty.'

Dryly, the Minister of Justice speaks on, but I no longer understand what he's saying . . . . As in a dream, in a well-defined rhythm, marking the passages of his speech, I see Kerensky's red handkerchief flashing up in the balcony.

I am tired . . . and is it any wonder? We haven't slept a wink since the 27th of February.

His voice rises to a crescendo — and it's over. He's finished. This time I hear his concluding words clearly.

'Obey your commanding officers. Long live Free Russia!'

'Hurrah! . . .' Hundreds of hands reach out to the new minister. His triumph is complete.

Slowly I walk out of the hall, savouring my fully earned right to leave. I am going home. Home — to sleep.

And all the while, as I walked down the streets alive with

people — each scurrying home and carefully nursing impressions of this historic night, like the candles from the Holy Thursday vespers — the thought of Kerensky's red handkerchief would not leave me alone. That handkerchief, which so unexpectedly, one may even say shamelessly found its way into the hands of the Minister of Justice, did not strike me as a banner of rebellion, but rather as a bloody signal, which the government raised up over the city on that long-ago day — as a sign that the country was now 'in a state of siege'.

Well, if that's the way it is then we shall fight . . . .
Indeed, 'Not enough blood has been shed.'

*Plate 7* Nicholas II — Emperor and Autocrat of All the Russias

# THE
# THIRD
# DAY

## The Arrest of Nicholas II
## by the
## Petrograd Executive
## Committee

9 March 1917

On the morning of 9 March, I reported as usual to my post in the military section of the Petrograd Soviet. Immediately I noticed its strangely empty appearance. From the very first days of the revolt we had always been besieged by crowds. The Soviet was still braced for battle, and even though its official rubric was 'The Soviet of Workers' and Soldiers' Delegates', *de facto* one could feel the power shifting, day by day ever more clearly, to the military section of the Soviet. The mass of soldiers felt the revolutionary break with the past order much more acutely than did the workers — who theoretically, at least, in their thoughts and songs, had turned their back on the past long ago. And if the workers, in view of their vastly greater experience in the political arena, having actively participated in the previous period of struggle, of victory and defeat, were more open to the idea of 'compromise' (for what is 'politics' if not the art of 'compromise'?), the soldiers were of a much more radical frame of mind. The compromise of 3 March, which raised the 'men of the Provisional Government' above the February barricades, remained 'a bad business' to the soldier at large. Psychologically they never accepted it, and the governing centre for the revolutionary garrison of Petrograd remained 'their' Soviet. It was here, and only here, that the soldiers, both male and female, came with all their thoughts, needs and suspicions. That's why there was always a crowd in the military section, at all hours of the day and night. A myriad of problems were brought before us, from the organization of the chain of command, to the question of officers' rights (down to whether officers could bear arms), and even to divorce proceedings and the baptism of children.

Both the scope and the number of such problems had expanded, day by day, which made the emptiness of the military section today, the tenth day of the revolution, even more unusual. I walked over to the rooms of the 'Union of Republican Officers' — the historic No. 41 and No. 42 — but there I only met a few officers on leave and the officer of the day.

'Where is everyone?'

'There was an emergency directive from the Executive Committee this morning, ordering everybody back to their units. We telephoned you, but you had already gone out.'

'Has anything happened?'

The officer on duty shrugged. 'I don't see how. Everything is quiet in the city. I just finished talking to the Preobrazhensky men and the Leib-Grenadiers. There's nothing new there.'

In the corridor I ran into the Secretary of the Executive Committee. As usual, he was all smiles and flying hair, the ends of his untied cravat bouncing along out of rhythm with his brisk walk. He grabbed me by my lapels: 'Why aren't you at the meeting?'

Even though the Executive Committee had been sitting in session almost continuously for these past days, the employees of the military section, myself included, seldom appeared at these meetings. These were devoted to 'high politics' — as they called their mad high-wire circus act, which involved carrying Miliukov on their shoulders and using Rodzianko for a balancing pole. As a member of the radical Left I considered these attempts to be literary exercises, having very little to do with reality. We could not sacrifice our precious working time with the soldier masses to these futile endeavours. We realized that the battle for the army's soul would take place shortly, and the result of this battle would decide whose side would be victorious, 'theirs' or 'ours', the Provisional Government or the Revolution. We went to Executive Committee meetings only in cases of dire necessity, in regard to specifically military section matters, to get approval from above, to get documents officially stamped, or as we put it 'to get them Chkheidzed'. The Executive Committee, for its part, left us alone. All of which meant that if today they requested our appearance at their meeting then 'something really big' was afoot.

The doors of Chkheidze's cabinet, where the extraordinary session was taking place, usually stand hospitably open. Today, in contrast, not only are they firmly closed but there's even a guard standing in front of them. Entrance is strictly forbidden to anyone outside the Executive Committee. This fact in itself is highly significant.

When we entered, the Executive Committee was already in full swing. There was a strange feeling in the air.

On the surface, everything seemed the same. N.D. Sokolov, his straggling beard spread out over his waistcoat, the pleats of his inevitable frock-coat uncreasing before our eyes, was proceeding with his current speech, which he had apparently begun quite a while back, in his usual theatrical manner. As ever, Sukhanov's yellow-grey, browless face smiled its dry and acid smile with strangly thick and bloodless lips. As usual, Filippovskii remained silent, attentive and, in the manner of the Navy, neat as a pin. And, as always, Steklov's massive figure both physically and psychologically overshadowed that of the thin, goateed and sandy-haired Skobelev.

Everything seemed the same but the atmosphere — which was very tense. Chairman Chkheidze's accent seemed extraordinarily noticeable, and his dark, tired eyes shone with a lurid light.

In an excited whisper my neighbour brought me up to date. Last night the Executive Committee was informed that the Provisional Government had decided to 'evacuate' the former Imperial family to England, including Nicholas II, who had just reached Tsarskoe Selo and been 'formally' placed under arrest. In order to avoid any 'incidents' on the way to Archangel, where the family was to board an English vessel (no doubt to the sounds of a twenty-four gun salute), Kerensky himself offered to escort them to safety. The whole farce of placing the royal family under arrest had been, as was to be expected, a mere subterfuge carried out to lull our suspicions.

Through this decision of the Provisional Government the question of the future fate of the dynasty, which now had to be faced by the Executive Committee, assumed a much more radical colour than had the parallel events faced by the great French Revolution in the days of Louis' flight to Varennes. At stake was not only the fate of the Imperial Family, but that of the Provisional Government itself; the 3rd of March compromise seemed about to collapse.

It was clear what Miliukov and Rodzianko had hoped to gain by this move; through this 'kidnapping' they counted on resolving the one issue closest to their monarchist (though not very loyal) hearts, i.e. Russia's future form of government. They had wished to force our hand, counting on that combination of 'low spirits and empty words' which had forced the leadership of the present Soviet to hand the power over to them in the first place. They were counting on the acquiescence of the Mensheviks in the Soviet Presidium and the coalition of Kerensky, Miliukov and Kornilov (who had just accepted the Petrograd district command) to secure the monarchy without authorization or opposition. For what other possible result could the flight to Archangel have than the restoration of the monarchy in the shortest possible period of time?

The abdication text was clear on that point; in order to invalidate it one did not even need the brave gesture of an oath-breaker. It was ambiguous enough to allow a perfectly 'legal' return to 'the throne of his ancestors'.

The counter-revolution had to keep 'the monarch' in the

game; regardless of how ineffectual he might be in real life. It was apparent to anyone who had had a chance to observe Nicholas II during the long years of his reign that here indeed was a true 'chess king', who could only be distinguished from a pawn by his 'inviolability'. . . . But at the first move of this crowned pawn, driven by the centuries-old rules of the game, the bishops, knights and rooks take up their accustomed places around the king. And if Great Britain, under whose familial roof the Romanovs were hurrying to take shelter, should also decide to turn her powerful and experienced hand to this game, it will be hard to reach a checkmate. In fact, judging from the present disposition of the pieces, we could easily lose before we have had the chance to bring all our forces into play. And then — the restoration would be inevitable.

But Rodzianko and Miliukov had, in their cleverness, miscalculated. A 'restoration' sounded too radical, even to a Menshevik Executive Committee . . . moreover, there was no doubt in anyone's mind what would be the reaction of Petrograd's revolutionary masses to the news that the Romanovs had been sent abroad to the centre of counter-revolutionary activity. The Provisional Government had miscalculated the blow. All of the orators who spoke during that session of 9 March were of a single opinion: the Revolution had to be secured from any possibility of a restoration. The Executive Committee had no choice but to respond to the challenge posed by the Provisional Government through its unilateral initiatives concerning the monarchy.

But what exactly would be our response? On that point all our orators reached a dead end. It became quite evident, throughout the many speeches that were given, that the age-old shadow of the throne — empty but not at all a dead letter — was still very much with us that day . . . .

The discussions concerning to what degree the monarch was personally dangerous, and which of the Grand Dukes should be placed in the category of 'threats' to the future Republic, grew ever more long-winded and confused as the day wore on. The gaze of the sharply anti-monarchist Executive Committee grew lacklustre and confused when confronted with the logical conclusion of their position concerning the fate of the dynasty. There were moments when the dreaded word 'regicide', so wounding to the Menshevik ear, seemed about to descend on the company from on high, in the manner of the tongues of flame at the Apostles' heads. . . . But, inevitably, at the decisive moment, a spasm of fear choked each orator, thus keeping the fatal thought from ever being uttered out loud. And once again a shimmering cloud of hints, innuendoes and half-truths would descend over the company.

Therefore, all sighed with relief when someone hurriedly proposed that debate now cease: 'The time is short, let's get down to business.' Chkheidze put a motion: 'Should the departure of the Tsar's family be permitted? Anyone against it?'

As one, all hands are nervously raised.

'In that case, it's necessary to take measures to prevent similar attempts, once and for all: the Provisional Government could, at the first convenient opportunity, try again. The Republic must be secured from the return of the Romanovs to the historical arena. Therefore, all the "dangerous" Romanovs must be in the hands of the Petrograd Soviet — in our hands, not in those of the "provisionals". Not with the "provisionals". . . .

'Any objections? More precise formulation? That's superfluous: further concrete action will be determined by the course of events themselves.'

And again, no objections were raised. We moved on to practical matters. The presiding committee informed us of the preliminary measures which it had undertaken earlier that morning. The entire complement of officers loyal to the Soviet (the Union of Republican Officers) has been mobilized. District detachments of armed workers are battle ready. All railway stations have already been occupied by the nearest military units under the command of commissars designated by the Executive Committee. Now, as a result of a decision made during the plenary session, and 'in accordance with its spirit' (Chkheidze's eyes flashed gloomily at this phrase), what was begun remains to be finished — in Tsarskoe Selo where the Tsar's family is situated. The detachment assigned to this task — the Semenovtsy and a company of machine gunners, for which its officers vouch with their lives, has already been dispatched to the Tsarskoe Selo railway station. The Executive Committee needs only to appoint a special emissary who will assume the command of this detachment and execute the decision just taken. N.D. Sokolov takes the floor again. He presents the qualities needed in such an emissary. Given such general and vague directives, any 'decision', practically speaking, will have to be made on the spot — and such a decision will determine the entire course of immediate political events. 'Under such circumstances, both impetuosity and indecisiveness are equally undesirable.' Today's assignment has to be accomplished 'at any cost'. The price, whatever it might be, 'must be calculated without a margin of error'. . . .

My neighbour, leaning towards me, is mumbling something unintelligible in my ear. I ask him to repeat it and at that moment I hear my name. I turn around. Sokolov proposes my candidacy. I feel the stares of the gathering upon me, guarded, searching . . . . Chkheidze is asking me whether I am willing to accept the assignment.

The Executive Committee voted. No one opposed or abstaining. 'Proceed immediately. Select the men you need and take action. You'll receive your orders right away. The car is waiting . . . .'

Whom should I take? All our officers are already dispersed among various railway stations and district soviets. As before, the Officers' Union is empty: I see only two or three men whom I remember from the 'first days'. Of these, Staff-Captain Tarasov-Rodionov, a machine gunner, volunteers to join me; another, Liubarsky, refuses, despite the fact that his

Semenovtsy company belongs to my detachment. Tarasov and I proceed alone. I feel that he is absolutely reliable; he is calm and likes danger. I was already sitting in the car when I received my written orders. The first set, which were addressed to me, stated: 'Upon receipt, immediately proceed to Tsarskoe Selo and claim all civilian and military powers for the execution of the extraordinarily important assignment delegated to you.' The second, addressed to the authorities in Tsarskoe Selo, requested their 'complete cooperation and assistance in the execution of this task of exceptional national significance'.

Surrounded by a tight circle of curious bystanders, a formation of Semenovtsy stood on the platform facing the main entrance of the railway station. Its officers were in attendance and a company of machine gunners was attached to its left flank. I greeted them briefly, as if on the front line. An abrupt, sonorous command and the rows double and close rank. The machine gunners, copper flashing on the cartridge belts which are crisscrossed on their chests, push the low-slung, grumbling machine guns up the stone steps. At the entrance Gvozdev meets us, wearing an enormous red rosette; he is a member of the Executive Committee (the future Minister of Labour). 'Everything's going according to plan: the telegraph and telephone stations have been taken; the station master and the commandant have been arrested without any resistance; your carriages have been attached to the next train, whose departure is being delayed. It can leave as soon as you're on board.'

Breaking formation and fixing their dark clanking bayonets as they go, soldiers scatter among the carriages. A chain of chausseurs who had originally secured the station are preventing curious bystanders from reaching our party. At the last minute, a certain nimble somebody, wearing a worn little coat with his collar turned up, slips through the guard and runs up to our window at the very moment when the train, without bells or whistles, slowly begins to pull out.

'Where are you going? Where to?' he desperately yells out, clinging to the rail on the platform, which overflows with soldiers. There is so much pleading and sincere despair in his outcry that from the platform and into the train a wave of smiles undulates across the soldiers' faces.
'Who are you? Where did you come from?'
'I'm from a newspaper . . . the correspondent of *The Russian Will.*'
'Ah, if that's the case then you can drop dead. . . . Let go, you riff-raff.' 'Hey you, tell them that the Semenovtsy are paying a visit to the Tsar. . . . If you don't watch out, you'll get it on the head with a rifle butt.'
The correspondent lets go of the rail, helplessly throwing up an arm as he trots along next to the rapidly accelerating train. . . . He disappears from sight. The soldiers continued to smile for another second. Then all smiles disappeared and their mood became sombre and strained. We rode without songs. The closer we got to Tsarskoe Selo the longer grew the soldiers' faces. They stared fixedly out of the windows at the striped mile poles quickly flashing past. Their voices were becoming hoarse — 'the throat's dry'. Outside, groves of fir trees and lonely birches shimmered in a frosty mist.
'You know,' one of the officers whispered with concern. 'We have almost no ammunition. The soldiers have about twenty cartridges each. They didn't want to take any more with them . . . their rifles aren't loaded. Only the machine gunners have complete sets.' And, after a brief silence: 'I hope things go without a hitch. If. . . .'
'Don't fret, they'll manage. If it becomes necessary. . . . But it's best not to make people nervous ahead of time. As far as the cartridges are concerned — if things go that far we'll get some at Tsarskoe, from the riflemen. There should be enough to go around.'

Tarasov-Rodionov suggests something along the lines of a military council. I decline his proposal: there's nothing to discuss. To me, the plan of action is clear. I'm giving the initial orders on the spot. The others will wait until our arrival. As we drew closer to Tsarskoe Selo, the hum of soldiers' voices subsided and finally ceased altogether. In the midst of a terrible, strained silence we pulled into the station. Crossing themselves, the soldiers fixed their bayonets. . . .

We disembarked quickly and smoothly. The Semenovtsy immediately cheered up and pulled themselves together when the machine guns rolled off the train and up the asphalt platform, racing each other and yelping with the rusty voices of their heavy little wheels. The telephone and telegraph were taken on the run, without difficulty. The station master, trembling from astonishment, instantly recovered upon being informed that his was not an 'official' arrest, and would consist only of his being under continuous observation by an officer assigned to this task. The detachment took up position in the third class waiting room and stacked its rifles.

The station master appeared to be forewarned. My request that he order a car, and immediately summon the commander of the garrison and the commandant of Tsarskoe Selo to the city hall prompted the astonishing reply that 'They are both already waiting there.'

I decided to go to the city hall alone, taking with me only Tarasov-Rodionov and two riflemen as liaison orderlies. I delegated my authority to the officer next in command, the commander of the Semenovtsy company, with an order to be ready should the local authorities, whose loyalties were unknown to us, attempt any sort of resistance. If I hadn't returned within the hour, or communicated with him by messenger or telephone, he was to proceed with the detachment to the barracks of the Second Infantry regiment (according to our information we could rely on their revolutionary fervour). Once there, he is to rouse the riflemen, take the palace, and carry out the mission delegated to us. 'At any cost,' I repeat emphatically, 'at any cost we must secure the revolution against the possibility of a restoration. Thus, depending on the circumstances, either remove the prisoners to Petrograd, into the Peter-Paul Fortress, or liquidate the question on the

*Plate 8* Russian soldiers in the period of the Revolution

spot in Tsarskoe. Whatever happens, it has to be done once and for all. Prior to departure, inform Petrograd by telephone. And please' — I say with a chuckle, 'do not call for reinforcements. Do, just for once, break this front-line tradition. In the meantime, see to it that the soldiers are fed.' I said all this as a matter of routine, just to maintain order. Had I doubted, even for a second, my certain, joyful, inner conviction that the detachment would not need to move from the railway station, I would never have transferred my command to anyone. As if missions of this sort could ever be delegated?

The station master approached us, accompanied by the officer assigned to watch him. 'The car is here.'

It was a small car, a two-seater. I got in with Tarasov-Rodionov. The liaison orderlies hop on the running boards. 'To the city hall!'

'The military powers' — two very upright, completely identical colonels (even their bald spots matched), in neatly buttoned jackets, with Vladimirs in their lapels — awaited me in a room on the second floor. The room was curtained off from the main hall with drapes, revealing herds of visitors milling around the desks of the section chief. I presented my orders. The colonels exchanged glances. 'To transfer command. . . . Now look here, you must excuse us, but we were sworn to uphold the Provisional Government, not the Petrograd Soviet. Since these documents do not have the official stamp of the Government they must have been drafted outside its authority.'

'That's not entirely true. But am I correct in concluding that you therefore do not accept the resolutions of the Soviet of the revolutionary garrison and the revolutionary workers of Petrograd?'

The colonels again exchanged glances and simultaneously began to fidget. 'Not at all! The Soviet has been recognized by the Provisional Government itself. . . . But, as a military man, you must understand that we can carry out the order only under a strict chain of command. We are under the command of General Kornilov, commander of this military district. Since your order contradicts the instructions given by the general, we cannot carry it out without breaking our military oath. However, we shall now attempt to communicate with him by telephone.'

'If I needed General Kornilov to carry out my mission, I'd have brought you more than his signature . . . . Leave Kornilov out of this. Especially since, by the powers of my mandate, I don't in the least intend to take orders from you. Only one thing is expected from you now: to take me to the former Emperor.'

'To the Emperor!' One of the colonels walked away with downcast eyes; the other, with a nervous gesture, stuck his hand under the broad lapel of his jacket. 'That's absolutely impossible. I was formally and most strictly forbidden even to name the palace in which His Majesty is situated to anyone.'

'Then you refuse . . . .' I continue.

'No, I don't refuse' — hurriedly the colonel shakes his head — 'but I must get General Kornilov's permission first.'

And so we have come a full circle once again.

'Listen here, gentlemen. You know, of course, that I am accompanied by a detachment. Instead of wasting time in futile conversation with you, I could simply have called on your garrison to rise. They would have joined me at the wave of a hand, after one call. The only consideration which keeps me from following this course of action is my firm belief that I will be able to accomplish this assignment by myself without any unnecessary unpleasantness, without unsheathing my sword. I shall do this solely by the power vested in me by the people, in the name of the people. With you, or without you, the task will be accomplished. The only remaining question is that of means, and these do depend on you. If you force my soldiers to take up arms, the blood which will flow will be on your hands. For the last time, where is the former Emperor?'

The commandant glanced at the garrison commander who,

in turn, glanced back at him.

'Don't you understand, we can't . . . our oath, our loyalty
. . . .'

'Time is running out. We must end it now. I only have an
hour at my disposal. You must either try and arrest me, or else
I shall arrest you.'

The officers looked up at me happily. A solution had been
found to their dilemma. 'We do not find it possible to arrest
you, since you are a representative of the Executive Committee.'

'Fine, then there's nothing more to discuss; gentlemen, you
are under arrest. And now I ask you, as my prisoners, where
is the former Emperor?'

'In the Alexander Palace . . . but they won't let you in
there, not even if you took us along. Direct orders from
Kornilov: without his personally written permission no one is
allowed to see the Emperor, not even the government
ministers.'

But I wasn't paying attention. Time was passing very
quickly. As I turned to leave I saw a telephone on the wall . . . .
Should I transfer the prisoners to another room? It would
only make the atmosphere that much tenser . . . even the
appearance of my two orderlies had caused a stir in the office.
I wanted our rear to be as calm as possible.

'I shall complete my assignment in an hour. I want you to
give me your word that during this time you will not touch
the telephone. I shall leave you behind in this room.'

Again, the colonels exchange glances. And answer as one:
'We give you our word.'

Tarasov-Rodionov sat, a prey to boredom, in the
automobile. I got in . . . . 'To the Alexander Palace — and
step on it, comrade chauffeur.'

The iron gates in front of the right wing of the palace were
shut tight. The guard, apparently recognizing the commandant's car, came to our call, gave the automobile a friendly
slap, but absolutely refused to let us pass. He had been strictly

forbidden to let anyone through — on pain of the firing squad. It was with great difficulty that I finally convinced him to call his superior officer. A young ensign, still very green, childishly pompous and excited as all youngsters in responsible positions tend to be, hurriedly confirmed the ban: 'No one and not under any circumstances.'

'I have come on a particularly important mission for the Petrograd Executive Committee. Do you expect me to show you my papers here, in this cold? Orders can't cover all circumstances. And, you will forgive me, Ensign, if I say that it's not you who should be telling me what to do, but the other way around.'

A few more moments of wavering — and the first, hardest step has been taken. We are inside the gate, in the outer guardhouse. Tarasov stayed in the automobile, 'just in case'.

I show the ensign my papers.

The youth is utterly confused. 'And what do you want me to do?'

'Take me through to the inner guardhouse.'

'But I had no right to let you come even this far. General Kornilov. . . .'

Again the sacrosanct name . . . . I remembered the general's sly face lurking behind the facade of 'simple soldier' at the last meeting of the Executive Committee and the General Staff, his ingratiating speech declaring 'what an honour it was to command the revolutionary troops who had been the first to throw off the yoke, etc. . . .' And yet, why was it that hidden in the depths of those seemingly kindly eyes I felt a tiger of rage, ready to spring?

'Kornilov's orders? . . . I am acting in the name of the Revolutionary Nation, therefore my orders supersede his. You will take me to the inner guards.'

'But I cannot desert my post . . . allow me to call the palace commandant.'

'All right, but not a word more than is necessary.'

A short pause followed. We wait. The ensign is nervously

adjusting his uniform. A corporal of the guard, standing in the doorway, is gloomily staring at either the floor or my boots.

After several minutes the commandant appears. Captain Kotsuba was a well-rounded fellow encased in a starched tunic: his buttocks jutted out from beneath the short-cropped Uhlan jacket. We introduced ourselves. The ensign gave his report and Kotsuba looked over my papers.

'To the inner guardroom — nothing of the sort. The ensign will answer for letting you get even this far. We are under strictest orders from the legal government. . . .'

'So, Captain, in your opinion the Soviet is not legal? The ensign will not answer for anything, but you, honourable commandant, just might have to. . . . You seem to be suffering from a short memory: only ten days have passed since the 27th of February.'

'But your . . . *comment dit-on* . . . Executive Committee . . . must understand that they have no right to place people in such an awkward position. . . . It was your own Soviet which recognized the Provisional Government, as we also recognize it. And yet you want us to disregard orders and start obeying the will of. . . .'

'Whose will, Captain?'

For an instant our glances met . . . and Kotsuba started to chew on his moustache nervously. I smiled.

'Shall I finish the phrase for you? It's not only a question of will, of course; the issue is where the actual power lies.'

The Uhlan glanced around the door.

'Don't worry. I am alone. The advance guard of the Revolutionary Petrograd Garrison which accompanied me here remains, for the time being, at the railway station. Well, shall we go?'

'I'll telephone Kornilov.'

'You will do nothing of the kind.'

Kotsuba jerked his head and slowly measured me with his eyes, from head to toe. Then he turned around and walked to the telephone.

I took a step forward. 'In that case, Captain, you are under arrest.'

The corporal in the doorway shuddered, straightened up, and froze. I heard the clang of rifles from the other side of the door.

Kotsuba stopped, looked at the captain of the guard and then at the lance corporal, chewed on his lips for a bit, shrugged his fat shoulders, and said through his teeth: 'Well, since you insist on using force, that's your affair. What can I do? Let's go.'

Through dark passages and crooked byways, past doors which had been nailed shut, past the grey figures of sentries, we made our way along a wide underground corridor. At last we heard voices again as we walked into a large room, dimly lit with electric lights, which was full of soldiers. Beyond the first room there was a second, just as crowded. At a rough estimate there must have been a whole battalion there.

'Greetings, comrades. Best wishes from the Petrograd Garrison and the Soldiers' Soviet.'

The barracks responded enthusiastically. The soldiers who were lying down get up to have a look, everyone crowds around the passageway. Kotsuba retracts his fat neck back into his tight collar and hurries on.

'Which regiment was that?'

'The Second Infantry.'

The game is ours.

I stopped. Instantly a crowd formed around me. Shortly and curtly, I explained my assignment to the soldiers — why the Soviet had sent me here. Immediately their eyes darkened, their brows came together, and I felt the hackles rise all around the formerly drowsy barracks.

'Peacefully, without bloodshed, comrades. But firmly: our sole criterion is the will of the people. Petrograd is depending on you — you see, I have come alone in order to pass the task on to you. Don't let us down.'

'You can count on us, comrade. It's a serious business —

don't we know it. Until we get direct orders from the Soviet we won't go off duty. And as long as we're on guard no one will get them out — not by force, and not by tricks either.'

Someone grabbed my arm. I turned around and saw a frowning and agitated lieutenant.

'What are you doing here? Come quickly — the officers are waiting for you.'

I followed him into a room where about twenty officers were crowding around Kotsuba, who was clearly enjoying his role of orator. They were all over-excited.

As soon as I entered they surrounded me in a close and threatening ring. Everyone was talking at once.

'What the hell do you think you're doing . . . this is unheard of . . . they had just calmed down, and now you have them riled up again.'

'Just a minute, gentlemen,' a solitary voice rose above the chorus. The speaker, a not very young lieutenant, seemed familiar to me. Then I recognized him: a Constitutional Democrat, one of their 'young leaders' whom I had occasionally met at inter-party conferences. He pulled me by the sleeve to a far corner of the room — behind some curtains.

'Do you recognize me? Do you remember me? In that case you know I can be trusted . . . . You are playing with fire. To murder the Emperor in his own palace, while he is in our custody — the regiment can't allow that to happen. If the commandants of the town and the palace let you through, let that be on their conscience . . . but our officers . . . .'

I laugh out loud. 'Do I look like Macbeth or Count Palin? Besides, regicide is more in the line of the Russian Guards regiments, isn't it? Why must you suspect every Socialist-Revolutionary of regicidal tendencies?'

'But Kotsuba says . . . .'

'Kotsuba can answer for what he says, just as I will bear responsibility for what I say.'

'According to him, you have a document which . . . .'

'Here is my document.'

'Kotsuba's right. It is ambiguous enough to be very

frightening. You have a mandate for regicide in your hands.'

'And more besides, if you like. However, the fact remains that Kotsuba is a liar. Gentlemen officers . . . .'

And I told them about the 'flight to Varennes' plan, and the decision of the Executive Committee. And the longer I spoke the calmer they became, with the exception of a few senior officers, who continued to be on edge.

'Let's suppose it's as you say . . . . But still, you must admit that forcing your way into the palace, alienating the troops from their commanding officers . . . . We know what's going on in Petrograd. What have you been telling our men?'

But the younger men interrupted this harangue, and quietened the captains down.

'You worried needlessly in the Executive Committee, you know. Our infantry has wholeheartedly gone over to the side of the Revolution. And yesterday, when the former Emperor arrived, we almost had to use force when it came to taking over guard duty. The Guards regiment didn't want to relinquish their tour of duty — yet we couldn't trust them, we knew where their sympathies lay. And we achieved our purpose. All of this, of course, makes your lack of confidence that much more insulting.'

'What "lack of confidence"! If we had doubted you, I wouldn't have appeared here alone, I'd have brought a whole division with me. We still have a few supporters in Petrograd and Kronstadt. But since the arrest can take place here, without transporting anyone to the Peter and Paul Fortress. . . .'

'We won't let you take "him" anywhere,' says an older captain gloomily, turning away from me.

'Please don't provoke me. As you yourself know perfectly well, he will go, you will go, and anyone else will go, if we decide it's necessary. But the Soviet would like this to be done quietly. That is why I wish you'd change your tone. After speaking to the soldiers, I don't believe a transfer to be necessary. At least for the moment. The men have promised to stay on duty until they receive orders from the Petrograd Executive Committee.'

They went over to the window to discuss my proposal, and a senior officer came back with their answer. 'In the name of the regiment, I give you my word that as long as we shall be on guard duty at this palace, neither the former Emperor, nor his family, will leave these walls. And we will do sentry duty with no outside relief, even if this means a month at arms, right up to the moment when we get other orders from the Petrograd Soviet. Does this satisfy you?'

'Quite. We only need to discuss the logistics of the matter.'

They bring a plan of the palace and its surrounding territory, with all the sentry stations marked; according to the plan the palace is protected by a triple chain of sentry posts and piquets. The right wing, in which Nicholas is staying, is completely isolated from the quarters of the former Empress and the children, in the left wing. No member of the former royal family, or of the staff, is allowed to leave the palace precincts. Anyone who enters the palace, even with the permission of the Provisional Government, automatically puts himself under arrest. There is no way back out of the palace for anyone. Even the doctor who is taking care of the sick children of Nicholas Romanov visits them under military escort.

'Don't worry, not even a mouse could get through.'

We had now come to the final act: an inspection of the guard. 'See for yourself, the trap has snapped shut.'

'Yes, but first I must make certain that the "beast" is indeed inside . . . you must show me the prisoner.'

The officer shuddered when I said this, and gloom descended on the company once again.

'Show you the Emperor . . . you? He will never agree to that.'

'What an idea! Why that's even worse than . . . .'

'Don't be embarrassed. Worse than regicide? You're absolutely right. And that is why I must insist on it.'

'An unnecessary cruelty,' a very young second lieutenant, neat as a pin, heatedly interrupts me. 'You know that there is no doubt whatsoever in your mind that he is here, inside these walls . . . . Are you saying that we are playing out a farce, guarding an empty palace? We have all seen him. We give you our word as officers and gentlemen that he is a prisoner here. Perhaps that's not enough for you? Perhaps you do not wish to accept our word of honour?'

Once again, their voices became threatening. And the peaceful conclusion to this episode, which had already seemed secure, started to slip away. For the more eloquently the officers tried to dissuade me, the clearer the value, the priceless value, of this symbolic gesture appeared to me. At first I had mentioned my desire to see the prisoner in passing,· almost mechanically, since it seemed absurd to return to Petrograd with a report without having seen the former Emperor in person. It was the reaction of the officers, the very passion with which they opposed my plan, which clarified my understanding of this problem. I then understood that this act of abasement — for yes, it was abasement — was absolutely necessary. I understood that the essence of my mission that day lay not so much in the arrest itself, as in this act. Arrests, imprisonments, or even the scaffold could never destroy autocracy. How many times in history monarchies had passed through various trials, and every time, like the phoenix, risen anew from the ashes of the funeral pyre, in all their splendour. No, we needed something else. This is what will make our 'Terror' so miraculously unique — we shall replace the old mysticism and mystery of 'God's anointed' with everyday physiology. And now, let Nicholas Romanov pass before me, by my orders, so that the whole world now entranced by the action taking place in our revolutionary arena will see him, the Emperor, 'the Autocrat of All the Russias' in the role of an ordinary arrested man being inspected in his cell . . . . That they will never forgive him, neither living nor dead.

I categorically demand to see the prisoner in person.

The officers felt my intransigence in this matter and finally called in Count Bekendorff, the Master of Ceremonies at court. If the officers had bridled at my demand, it is easy to imagine how it affected the old man. He literally started foaming at the mouth, and in the first few moments could not utter a single word. 'You wish to "inspect" His Majesty . . . what insolence . . . and who are you, a mere rebel! Let us call things by their proper names.'

He absolutely refused 'to even inform His Majesty about this'.

And the various protestations started again. I took out my watch. 'Soon it will be an hour since I left the station, where my detachment awaits me. If the hour passes before I can inform its commander that my mission has been accomplished, this will serve as a signal. The Semenovtsy will then proceed to the palace — and Petrograd will in its turn send troops to Tsarskoe Selo, to support my advance guard. The fate of the Provisional Government, of the former dynasty, finally of all Russia, will once again be left hanging by a thread. And is there any question whose side will ultimately win? The real power is in our hands. Just listen to your underground barracks. Can't you see that I need only unsheathe my sword, and they'll follow me to a man? And the responsibility for what will occur then lies squarely on your shoulders; I have done all I could to avoid shedding blood. Don't waste time needlessly. You cannot hold back the wheel of history: you'll only break your fingers if you try.'

A new delegation goes off to try and convince Bekendorff. This time, after a brief struggle (I was watching the minute hand on my watch), the Master of Ceremonies, in his turn, 'gave in to brute force'. 'I will, of course, register his protest with the highest authorities, with the Provisional Government, with General Kornilov. You will pay dearly for this.'

'With pleasure. But let's get on with it.'

We go over the arrangements. The Emperor will appear before me in the inner chambers, where two corridors meet; he will pass by me, not meeting me face to face. I laughed from the bottom of my heart. 'Certainly, certainly, if this cotillion will make it easier to bear.'

While they were 'preparing the monarch for inspection' I telephoned the station to confirm my imminent arrival. I also telephoned the outer guard house, to tell them to let Tarasov-Rodionov through. Actually, it turned out that they had let him in long ago, and that at that moment he was peacefully dining with the captain of the guards.

The captain of the inner guard accompanied me on my 'inspection'. They spent a long time, conspicuously long, in unlocking the door, which was locked both by a huge hanging lock, and with a key. A heavy guard was standing by this door; inside the sealed palace itself there wasn't a single soldier. This was a highly rational measure for it prevented, once and for all, any communication between the prisoners and the outer world, which inevitably would have occurred if the 'prisoners' had had any contact with their guards. For, as experience shows, there isn't a guard who will not eventually succumb to temptation — either through pity, or respect, or greed . . . . But, under this arrangement, Nicholas Romanov was literally buried alive — with his cooks and his lackeys — completely, and without the slightest access to the outside world.

But inside this cage the Provisional Government had left everything alone — the way it had been before the catastrophe, in the heyday of the 'Grand Imperial Palace', with all of its luxuries, with all of its rituals. When we finally entered through the grumbling doors, squeaking on their hinges, a fantastic crowd of courtly retainers surrounded us — respectful, but curious. A huge coachman — an exact replica of Trubetskoi's statue of Aleksander III — in a bearskin hat; messengers; court moors in gold-embroidered red velvet coats, turbans and slippers with upturned toes; outriders in tri-cornered hats and red mantles stamped with imperial eagles — they all crowded around us. Silently moving over the soft carpets, footmen ran ahead of us in their patent leather slippers to the 'inner chambers'. All of this seemed doubly bizarre against the background of our 'prosaic' revolutionary experiences of the past few days. Everything continued as usual in this vast structure, which seemed to have muffled even the most distant echo of the revolutionary storm which had criss-crossed our country from one end to the other.

And when, having ascended the staircase, we 'proceeded' through reception rooms, banquet halls, waiting rooms; as we walked over carpets which muffled the brazen ring of my spurs, and gleaming parquet floors, in turn — we could see, in each room, its particular set of footmen, dressed in the particular costumes which matched the room's colour scheme. We saw footmen dressed in the traditional black coats and tails; in white, red or black shoes and stockings; in wildly exotic eastern costumes . . . .

In the upper hall, which had been converted into a portrait gallery, beneath a glassed-in roof a small group of courtiers awaited us, headed by Bekendorff. Kotsuba, who had somehow found his way in during our 'negotiations', was also there. The courtiers were dressed completely in black, their frock-coats buttoned up to their chins. About six steps away from our meeting place there was an intersection with another corridor; this was where the former Emperor would walk past me.

I stopped in the middle of this corridor, Bekendorff to my right, Dolgorukii and another unfamiliar civilian to my left. The officers who had accompanied me stood a few steps behind us.

Bekendorff could not control himself any longer and began to whisper angrily in my ear. (Here everybody talked softly, because 'His Majesty deigned to be present in the neighbouring rooms'.) He said something about lese-majesty, and that it was only due to the extreme indulgence of the monarch, only his sincere desire to do everything within his power to calm his deluded but loyal — no matter what they say to the contrary, still loyal — subjects, which forced him to honour my request, a request so appalling that he, Bekendorff, could personally find no words to describe it. My name was familiar to him. He had known my father, and still remembered my grandfather. 'And how could you, with your family's past, how could you take upon yourself such an act of lese-majesty . . .! If it had been someone from among those parvenus in the Tauride Palace, some 'idze' or other . . . . But you! And in such a state!'

Actually my appearance was rather 'Razin'esque', for I had not had a chance to change my clothes since the day of the revolt. I was unshaven, wearing a sheepskin coat stuck all over with pieces of straw, a Cossack hat on my head, my uncombed hair sticking out under it. And the butt of my automatic was sticking awkwardly out of my side pocket; Dolgorukii could hardly keep his eyes off it.

Somewhere off to the side a door squeaked melodiously. Bekendorff fell silent, and with a trembling hand patted down his grey sideburns. The officers stood at attention, hurriedly buttoning their gloves. We heard the sound of steps rapidly approaching us, and the faint jingle of spurs.

He was bareheaded, wearing a leib-hussar's khaki tunic. Nervously twitching his shoulders and rubbing his hands together, as was his habit, he stood at the point where the two corridors intersected, facing us. His face was puffy and red, his swollen eyelids forming a heavy frame for his dull, bloodshot eyes. For a moment he stood there, indecisively, then slowly, he came towards us. It seemed as though he was about to speak. Our eyes locked; he drew ever closer, step by step. A dead silence hung over the room. The still yellow gaze of the Emperor, so like that of a tired, hunted wolf, suddenly flickered with a flame which broke to the surface of its leaden indifference. It was a spark of deadly malice. I felt the shudder which passed through the officers standing behind me. Nicholas paused, shifted from foot to foot, and sharply turned around, walking rapidly away, twitching his shoulders, and limping.

Freeing my right hand, which had been tucked into my belt, I saluted the courtiers, and started on my way back, accompanied by a cloud of spittle from the indignantly spluttering Bekendorff. My fellow officers were sombrely quiet. It was

only in the vestibule that one of them turned to me, shaking his head reproachfully: 'You really should have taken off your hat. The Sovereign apparently had wanted to say a few words to you, but when he saw how you were standing. . . .'
And another added: 'Well, watch out now. If the Romanovs ever get back into power they won't forget you; they'll find you at the bottom of the sea, if need be . . . .'
'And how did you like old Bekendorff? What can one say, he's certainly a loyal old cuss.'

At the station they greeted me with undisguised, noisy joy. The 'liberated' telephones rang out happily, as if making up for enforced silence. The station master, red and impossibly talkative, got our train ready. The soldiers, picking up their rifles for the trip back, emphatically snapped their triggers, as if to laugh at their uselessness. And now we travelled to the sound of full-throated singing. The proverbial mountain had been removed from our shoulders. It was a wonderful feeling to sit back in that stuffy car, blue with the smoke of cheap tobacco, looking at the kindly eyes of the Semenovtsy, which only that morning had been so bleak . . . . Tarasov-Rodionov gave a mouth-watering description of the palace kitchen, which he had managed to visit, and of the tasty delicacies which the 'arrested crowned heads' were even now enjoying.

It was evening before I managed to reach the Executive Committee; on the way I had to stop at the Warsaw and Baltic Stations, to remove the guards we had posted there. The first report was given by Tarasov-Rodionov, who hopped on an armoured truck bound for Tauride Palace as soon as we disembarked at the station. I only had to fill in some factual and stylistic details — his report was of necessity an outline, since he himself had not entered the palace proper. Skobelev, who chaired the meeting, offered me his thanks, in the name of the Executive Committee as a whole, and informed us that the Provisional Government had agreed to place the prisoners under 'an accredited commissar of the Executive Committee' 'for the arrest and imprisonment of persons belonging to the former royal family'. He immediately offered me a commission for this position, expressing the hope that I 'would continue the task begun on 9th March in the same manner as . . . etc., etc.'

The Mensheviks had never been known for their psychological acumen or keenness of wit. Skobelev was sincerely surprised when I refused their 'honour' point blank. Neither he nor Chkheidze understood that to go to Tsarskoe Selo, as we did on 9th March, and to be 'the commissar in charge of the prisoners' were two entirely different things . . . .

I did however take along my commission, as a souvenir for the lads.

A day later the official Soviet release concerning the events of 9th March appeared. I hardly recognized my trip: they described how the palace was surrounded 'by a solid chain of armoured vehicles, machine guns and artillery pieces' and more nonsense in the same vein . . . . 'Why did you do this?' I demanded in all simplicity from the author of the release. 'You know very well that I walked that whole road alone, all alone, solely "in the name of the Revolution".'

'What are you talking about? It's much more effective this way. We're dealing with the masses, you know. Your version is pure romanticism, which may be fine for young ladies reading novels, but will not do for soldiers and workers . . . .'

*Plate 9* Detachment of sailors from Kronstadt in the October Revolution

# THE FOURTH DAY

## The October Revolution

25 October 1917

It was eight o'clock in the morning when I heard the cheerful tapping of rifles on my bedroom door.

'Get up, sleeping beauty. We've already taken the Government Bank.'

Recognizing the voices as the comrades from the Kronstadt organization, I opened the door.

'Why are you here?'

They all crowded in together, both familiar and unfamiliar faces. They had a certain unmistakable look about them: even-keeled, smiling, happy, and armed to the teeth. They radiated life. They were laughing.

'We came for some salt.'

'What salt?'

'Why to sprinkle on Kerensky's tail. So that he won't fly away . . . .'

'And so that he'll stop squawking,' added one of the older sailors, a short, squat, red-head with a beard which came right up to his clear, kindly, grey eyes.

'What are you fellows up to? What about the resolution?'

(A few days prior to this incident, I had gone over to Kronstadt at the request of the local Party organization, and it was there, during a Party conference after a meeting in the Naval riding school, that a unanimous resolution was passed: not to support any Bolshevik attempt at a takeover until the Congress of Soviets has had a chance to meet.) 'The resolution? The resolution is one thing, but the revolution is another. Gird up your loins, boss. There's a smell of gunpowder in the city.'

Actually, the city did not smell of gunpowder; power lay in the gutter, anyone could pick it up. One did not have to gird one's loins, one needed only to stoop down and pick it up. . . .

In reality, from those first March days the Provisional Government had gone into an obvious and rapid decline. Its doom was apparent from the time of the April and May crises which led to the premiership of Kerensky as the last chance for the bourgeoisie. The unfortunate attempt to graft the Chernov-Avksentiev type of socialism on to a Miliukov trunk only hastened, as might have been expected, the process of disintegration in the March 3rd 'tree of liberty'. In the decisive battle for the Army between the 'right' and the 'left' Kerensky, with his bizarre staff of socialist-revolutionaries and arch-conservative guards officers, lost with dizzying speed. After the June offensive, however, which could be viewed as a sporadic attempt on the part of the premier to shore up his crumbling political coalition, this disintegration assumed catastrophic proportions. At the moment of the Kornilov adventure, Kerensky was already a dead man politically. And since he was the alpha and omega of the March government to begin with, his crisis and his catastrophe naturally became the crisis and catastrophe of the Provisional Government as a whole.

In direct relation to this, the influence of the Bolsheviks on the masses grew ever more swiftly and surely, for the Bolsheviks were the only revolutionary group which advocated from the start the twin slogans of a 'realistic peace' and the 'expropriation from the expropriators' — the logical aim of a Social Revolution carried to its conclusion. Their propaganda activities gained a definite edge with the arrival of Lenin, who first appeared at the 1 May* Peasant Deputies Conference where he advocated a motion 'to pluck the capitalists' and instead of the 'land reform nonsense', which in his words 'came complete with statistics and other such tricks', simply told them to take the land.

Actually, the 'older' socialist parties managed to stave off Lenin's first attack on the peasantry. I remember the commotion in the Executive Committee raised by the news of Lenin's speech at the peasant conference, brought to us by a breathless assistant of Chkheidze straight from 'the field of battle'. The Mensheviks searched high and low for a 'champion' to send into battle against the 'Saracen' Lenin — the main criterion for choosing this champion being a certain glibness, since Lenin was a rather heavy opponent in debate, while the 'labouring peasantry' had a tendency towards irreverence . . . . Torn between Bogdanov and Skobelev, they finally gritted their teeth and settled on Maria Spiridonova . . . . The conference, in the words of Chkheidze, 'barely pulled through', but the peasants remained with the populists. In the army, however, the slogan of immediate peace and 'fraternization' quickly took the ground from under the feet of Kerensky's committees and commissars. The ideas of Bolshevism also evoked a similar response in working class neighbourhoods. In short, by autumn, the basic slogan of the Leftist, revolutionary wing of the movement, 'All Power to the Soviets', had become the true battle cry of the masses, who were still awaiting their revolution. The February revolt had not changed their position in the least: it had given them neither peace, nor bread, nor land, nor freedom; and due to its relative bloodlessness, it had done nothing to discharge their revolutionary energy, which had been accumulating over many years. And Lenin, who was very sensitive to precisely these sorts of tensions, hurried his Central Committee to 'finish it'. 'Let's stop wasting time,' he wrote during the days of the 'Democratic Conference'; 'we should simply surround the

---

* Mstislavskii probably confused the dates here. Lenin actually made the speech on 22 May.

Alexander Palace, scatter all the riff-raff, and take the power into our own hands.' The Central Committee, however, with the memory of the 'July days' still fresh in their minds, did not agree with 'Il'ich'. This in no way discouraged Lenin, who on his own initiative moved from Finland and exile to Petrograd. There, without wasting any more words, he began organizing his revolt — regardless of any 'considerations of strategy', incidentally, for he published whole articles on the subject in the newspaper.

We, of the then Left wing of the Socialist-Revolutionary Party, felt the quickening of the revolutionary pulse of the land no less keenly than Lenin. It was symptomatic that so many workers from the populist organizations, from Chernov's centre fraction (I don't even mention the Right here, since it had long ago been driven from the field), and from provincial party committees, who 'had their ear to the ground', came over to our side. We felt this pulse in our ever growing network of contacts with both the workers and the peasantry.

On the other hand, we had an even clearer view than the Bolsheviks of the degree to which government power was disintegrating. We were there, behind the scenes, during those 'government acts' which the Bolsheviks could only observe at a distance, sitting in the audience. In those days we were still in the very bosom of 'the ruling party'. Though not in the position of favourite sons, of course, and suffering under double surveillance by both the police and the party, we nevertheless had access to the building of the Central Committee; we still participated, as delegates, at meetings; in other words, we could both 'see' and 'comprehend'. And, consequently, from what we both saw and understood, both the leadership and the masses were telling us one and the same thing: the March government was finished; it was rotting like three-day-old fish and stinking . . . . And since this was the case, then the power, unified and undivided, had to go to the Soviets.

We were so sure of the utter inability of the Provisional Government to offer any resistance to the transfer of power to the labouring masses, as represented by the Worker-Peasant

Soviets, that despite our official October 7th coalition with the Bolsheviks, cemented after they withdrew from the 'Soviet of the Republic', we stepped forward in unambiguous and absolute opposition to Lenin's doctrine of revolt. Revolt — an 'appearance', a highly visible violent takeover — seemed from our point of view to complicate the whole situation needlessly. Such a takeover would rupture all ties with the bourgeoisie, including its most radical elements (i.e. the Right Socialist parties), and would inevitably carry us from the sphere of class (i.e. social struggle) into that of a civil (i.e. political) war. This would once and for all drive our movement back into the blind alley of the old form of government, upon whose threshold we had been poised ever since the degeneration of the Soviets began under Kerensky's leadership. In the case of a bloody rupture, such as Lenin advocated, victory in the difficult political battle which lay ahead would depend on one of two necessary conditions: either a radical break, a complete rejection of the whole government apparatus as we knew it, and thus neither war nor revolt; or the opposite approach — a firm emphasis on government of the most far-reaching sort, which naturally could not be built upon ruins. The 'anti-government' approach was inimical to the Bolsheviks: thus, their hegemony would automatically assure the victory of the second way. And, by this very fact, one could already foresee that the old petit-bourgeois model of government, now held hostage in our hands, rather than being dissolved, would have to be strengthened . . . strengthened exactly in those same old-fashioned typical forms, for anything 'new' could only be built on a debris-free foundation. And since a radical uprooting of the whole system was beyond our means — owing to political and military considerations — we were inevitably drawn back into the charmed circle of using the old government apparatus which we had, in words at least, rejected.

The whole system of soviets, in its essence, was both anti-political and anti-governmental (in our understanding of these two terms). Under the conditions then prevailing it was unrealizable as a political system, 'a dream fading away into the mist of the future', while the parties who had instigated the revolt were themselves condemned to 'governmental' degeneration; it was inevitable that they should lose their revolutionary essence before the real, social revolution had had a chance to take place.

Therefore the conclusion seemed clear: the Far Left should not take over government power unilaterally under the circumstances then prevailing. To persist on this course would be tantamount to suicide. For the dirty work of this 'transitional period' — the elementary solution of the political question at hand, in preparation for the transition to a truly soviet system — it was necessary, or so we thought, to make use of the Right Socialist parties, whose activity would be fuelled by the unremitting pressure of the revolutionary masses led by the Bolsheviks and Left Socialist Revolutionaries. They would perish, eventually, while performing this service, and on their bones would arise a new and real (and I emphasize this word) Soviet political Order.

I do not know whether this was the correct analysis of the situation or not, but at that time, those were our views. In consequence, the logical thing was to make a definite stand against Lenin's appeal for an immediate uprising.

Our speeches seemed 'doomed', however, even to ourselves. It's true that during meetings the soldiers and the workers applauded our orators, but one could feel that they were applauding the voices and the sounds as such, not their actual meaning; they kept their true thoughts to themselves. And what chance did all our discussions on the 'governmental system', 'the social priorities', and 'transitional periods' have against these thoughts, especially when contrasted with the simplicity and sonorous power of Lenin's battle cry? As I myself wrote in the *Banner of Labour* of 21 October, only four days before the revolt — 'It is difficult for the masses, for the masses in their current state, utterly exhausted by their consciousness of a "dead end", to stand firm against the temptations of a slogan which so simply, so radically offers to solve all our problems, all our difficulties, all our vexed questions. You want peace? — Rise up! And tomorrow you'll have peace. You want a world revolution? — Rise up! And tomorrow the world revolution will flare up in an awesome firestorm. You want bread? Rise up! And tomorrow you'll have bread. You want land? Rise up! And tomorrow you'll be the masters of the land. In brief — one short moment of decisiveness, of enthusiasm, one last, tense moment of street fighting — and we shall cross, finally, that last fatal boundary, that boundary which we have been edging towards in indecision for the last eight months.'

We, the Left wing of the Socialist-Revolutionary Party, had nothing with which to outbid these slogans. And so the Bolsheviks became the undisputed masters of the situation. The Northern District, its soviets and its garrisons, including the Petrograd troops, were totally under their control. Thus, both the front and the rear of our strategic arena was in their hands. On 10—12 October the Northern District Soviet Congress solemnly swore to give its full support to the approaching revolt.

On 21 October, during an emergency general meeting of the Petrograd garrison's regimental committees, everyone wholeheartedly approved the resolution concerning 'the formation of a battle-ready Revolutionary Army Committee', the first military organ of the newly-emerging, purely Soviet government, and promised it their help in all future endeavours. The 22nd of October, 'Petrograd Soviet Day' was celebrated on a wave of enthusiasm, with many thousands of people participating in the meetings. In the House of the People, Trotsky succeeded in charging up his audience to such a pitch that thousands raised their hands simultaneously, swearing an oath of allegiance to the Revolution — to defend it, and fight for it, if need be until death.

Kerensky watched this new storm rising among the masses, that elemental force which he longer controlled, with the eyes

of a cornered wolf. Ever since the 'July days', when he had
signed orders for the arrest of his most prominent 'Left-
leaning' party comrades, Kerensky no longer felt the need to
stand on ceremony with us. During our discussions his lips
would curl angrily around the word 'Rabble! . . .' If only he
had had the means, with what voluptuous pleasure would he
have watched the bloody trail of government troops cutting
their way into the crowds of 'mutinous slaves', and 'rebellious
mobs' as Victor Chernov, Minister of Agriculture, well-
known talker and coiner of phrases (now no less at sea than
Kerensky) called them, hissing from his corner. But they
didn't have the means; in Petrograd, Kerensky at best could
count only on the Cossack Regiments (the First, the Fourth,
and the Fourteenth), and he had their allegiance only on the
basis of Russian government tradition, not for any more
substantive reason. The former 'support' of Rodzianko — the
cadet military academies — remained as reactionary as ever,
but tactically their position was very unfavourable. They
were scattered among the barracks of troops loyal to the
Revolutionary Military Committee, so they could already be
considered as good as paralyzed. The RMC could liquidate
them at any time, with a single blow. The troops stationed in
the countryside of Peterhof/Gatchina, or Tsarskoe Selo? . . .
The tsarist government had placed its confidence in them
eight months ago, as it retreated to the Winter Palace . . .
mistakenly so. Could Kerensky forget this, as he too
retreated, with his government and his troops, towards the
Winter Palace in the days of his October sunset?

Nevertheless, he gave the order for the most trustworthy of
these troops to march on Petrograd; the shock battalion from
Tsarskoe Selo, the artillery from Pavlovsk, the officer
academy at Peterhof . . . . In reaction to his challenge, the
Revolutionary Military Committee, without losing a minute,
gave the signal to attack.

The sailors, the Guards, the Red Guards especially, burned
with enthusiasm for the task before them. If July was their
'Narva' [Peter I's famous defeat in the struggle for the Baltic]

then after 'Narva' it was the turn of 'Poltava' [Peter's decisive victory against the Swedes in 1709].

At about 2 a.m. on 25 October, troops of the Revolutionary Military Committee occupied the railway terminals and bridges, the electric station and the telegraph . . : . Kerensky called upon the Cossacks to step forward 'in the name of the liberty, honour and glory of our native land, and to the aid of the Central Executive Committee of the Soviets, of revolutionary democracy, of the Provisional Government and of perishing Russia'. But the Cossacks refused. 'If the artillery was on our side, it would be a different matter altogether, but without the artillery it's no go for us.' They stayed neutral. The Pavlovsk Academy also announced its intention of staying neutral, using as an excuse the close proximity of the Grenadier regiment, which had sworn loyalty to the RMC and had already fixed its bayonets. Thus, there were no reinforcements from outside Petrograd. Neither did the armoured vehicles heed the call of the government — even though, as we later found out, through some misunderstanding Kerensky had been counting on their support. Most declared their allegiance to the revolt, the rest remained neutral. By 7 a.m. the telephone exchange was in the hands of the RMC, and the lines to the Staff headquarters of the Petrograd District were immediately cut. All defensive manoeuvres thus became impossible. Kerensky jumped into an automobile to escape the steel trap which was closing on him. And he got out at the last possible moment; the Kronstadt sailors were already disembarking on the Nicholas Quay 'to try and sprinkle his tail with salt' as he left . . . .

At ten o'clock in the morning the Revolutionary Military Committee published a communique concerning the state of the rising:

To the Citizens of Russia!

The Provisional Government has been overthrown. Government power has been transferred into the hands of the Revolutionary Army Committee — an organ of the Petrograd

Soviet of Workers' and Soldiers' Deputies, which represents
the proletariat of Petrograd and the Petrograd Garrison.
The goals demanded by the people — the immediate implementation of a democratic peace, the abolition of the
private estates of the gentry, workers' control over the means
of production, and the creation of a soviet form of government
— have been secured at last. Long live the workers', soldiers'
and peasants' revolution!

As I've said, the city did not 'smell of gunpowder', despite
the revolt. Even the Soviet of the Republic, on 24 October,
refused to 'authorize' repressive measures against the
Bolshevik newspapers, abandoning Kerensky. The Central
Executive Committee, which was completely under the
thumb of Gotz, Libber and Dan, had a final emergency
session during the night of the 25th. They could do little
more, however, than wring their hands. Abram Gotz, the
unseen puppet master of their little theatre, whose voice
could be heard in the Menshevik and Socialist-Revolutionary
babblings, pulled on his various strings in vain. The SR Central
Committee had done everything possible, during Kerensky's
time, to destroy an influence they may once have had, and now
they were reaping what they had sown. On that fatal night
they were repugnant to everyone, including themselves . . . .
Who else was left? The municipal government? But the city
fathers, at the first news of the revolt, had hurried over to the
Soviet, to ask the victors their intentions. Having received
Trotsky's assurance that they, personally, were in no danger,
and that even if a place in the new soviet order could not be
found for the City Duma, its end would be quite 'constitutional' and without any excesses, they heaved a sigh of
relief. It was obvious that to do battle was the last thing on
their minds.
Kerensky fled — 'to get reinforcements', as the written
accounts always say. The other Provisional Government
ministers, who had not had time to follow his good example,
rushed about the city looking for a place to hide from the
armoured vehicles which were briskly patrolling all their old

*Plate 10*  A factory meeting, 1917

haunts. Finally, they found shelter in the Winter Palace, which had been occupied by one thousand cadets and a terrified women's battalion, who had been called out for a parade and instead found themselves embroiled in far trickier business.

The All Russian Congress of Soviets was supposed to open that day, its quorum present. Already that morning 663 delegates had registered, a number which surpassed our highest expectations since this Congress was under a semi-boycott from the Right Socialist parties. But despite the quorum, the session was not opened on time: the Bolsheviks wanted to present the Congress with a *fait accompli* by liquidating the Provisional Government before the opening session.

On their side, the various factions at the Congress were also in no hurry; they had a lot of decisions to make, serious decisions concerning their future strategy, in the light of unfolding events.

This question assumed a particularly acute form for us on the Left of the Socialist-Revolutionary Party. Despite the incredible tension of the party's 'internal relationships', we were still, officially, a unified whole. Thus, we were represented by one delegation at the Congress. And, since we were sure that at the grassroots the party had actually drifted much further Left than its leadership, which had remained frozen in the February scheme of things, we had a dim hope of tearing our delegation, and consequently the whole party, out of the hands of the Central Committee, and bringing it back into step with revolutionary events.

I only took over the leadership of our fraction halfway through the day; it was noon by the time I freed myself from various affairs in the city and showed up at the Smol'nyi Institute. The membership of our delegation left very little to be desired: the Far Right, 'the Zenzinovtsy', numbered no more than fifteen people; the overwhelming majority of the delegates were clearly in our camp; the 'centrists' were wavering; while the 'national' Socialist-Revolutionaries, the Jewish 'Sickle' and the Lithuanians, were definitely leaning towards the Left. The party's attitude towards its Central Committee was decidedly lukewarm. This was so evident that as chairman I allowed myself the luxury of making the members of the Central Committee — Gotz, Zenzinov and others — 'wait their turn' for a good hour, during which time our debates continued, before allowing them to present their reports. The fraction did not support the official protest lodged by the Right against such obvious 'disrespect to their rank'.

The Central Committee itself could feel that the atmosphere was unfavourable to it. Therefore, they did not enter into battle on the basic issue of our relationship to the transfer of power; on that score their policy was one of silent acquiescence. Instead, the Central Committee shifted the weight of our discussion to the question of the future membership of the central government; would it be homogeneously socialist, as we demanded, or would the 'February coalition' continue, an alternative favoured by the Committee? But even this point of view, so strangely divergent from the political reality of the revolutionary moment, was very tamely defended by them. One felt that they basically distrusted our whole delegation, despaired of converting us to their point of view, and were firmly promoting a policy which would result in a party split. Nevertheless, right up to that evening, I continued to hope that the unity of the party could be maintained, mainly because our opponents, helplessly mumbling their protests, seemed incapable of carrying through a split.

Towards evening I had to leave for an hour. Upon my return to the Smol'nyi I found the Right and Left fractions sitting in two separate rooms. And — the irony of fate! — the Right (the name was now official) was headed by Filippovsky, the man with whom I had raised the alarm on the very first night of the Revolution.

At 10.45 p.m. the Congress of Soviets opened at last,

beneath the blazing lights of ancient crystal chandeliers in the large assembly hall of the Smol'nyi, filled up to the very rafters with people, both 'ours' and 'theirs'. There was no longer any reason to put it off. The different delegations had decided upon their policies: we knew that the Right Socialists, who were now an insignificant minority, would boycott the Congress regardless of its proposed programmes or tactics. On the other hand, the 'military operations' in the city were also drawing to a close. The Provisional Government had at last been discovered hiding out in the Winter Palace, the Palace had then been cordoned off, and the *Aurora* was already moored just beneath its windows. The long-recalcitrant batteries of the Peter and Paul Fortress were trained at last upon this veritable tomb of Kerensky's government . . . . It certainly wasn't within the power of the women's battalion to deflect the blow which was even now being aimed at the palace by Podvoiskii and Antonov. . . .

The session was opened by Dan, the Menshevik, in recognition of his seniority, and in the name of the old Central Executive Committee of the Soviets. In his introductory speech one could hear the obvious echo of the funeral oration given by him less than twenty-four hours before, during the 'farewell' emergency meeting at the Tauride Palace.

'This is not the time for political speeches . . . . Our comrades in the Winter Palace are even now under fire . . . .'

He sounds dully resigned to his fate. And, involuntarily, breaking up the tension of the moment, a light laugh makes its way around the hall. And was it any wonder, the picture which Dan's words evoked was so vivid — that nest in which Kishkin and Tereshchenko, pale with fear, huddled together on the gilded couches of the former imperial rooms, eyes tightly shut . . . under the protection of women! Actually, it was both funny and repugnant . . . .

'I propose that we turn to the election of the Presidium.'

Avanesov steps up to the podium with a list in hand.

Lenin . . . Zinoviev . . . Kamenev . . . Lunacharsky . . . Kolontai . . . Spiridonova. . . .

As I, along with the other members of the newly-elected Presidium, climb to the hurriedly constructed podium, which sags beneath the weight of the people crowding upon it, we can hear the dull boom of the Peter and Paul battery. Immediately cheers and applause swirl through the festive hall in a triumphant wave.

Dan was replaced as chairman by Kamenev, whose joyous mood caught perfectly the spirit of the moment. And though he was wearing his ubiquitous jacket, worn and shiny around the seams, he seemed dressed in his 'Sunday best' that day.

'The Order of the Day . . . .'

'The question of the organization of the government . . . .'

'Of war and peace . . . .'

'The Constituent Assembly . . . .'

'Any objections?'

Again, a dull, distant boom, which sets our teeth on edge. Abramovich, a delegate from the Bund, is dancing around on the platform, as if in horrible pain: 'How can you expect any objections, at a time like this!'

'The representative of the Petrograd Soviet has the floor.'

The 'opposition', however, had no intention of hearing him out. They bombarded the chair with impatient proposals, without any attempt to maintain even a semblance of order. Kamenev seemed equally benign to all, nodding and smiling slyly from beneath his naturally lowering brows, writing away, keeping track of requests for the floor, writing in rhythm to the sharply clipped words of the speaker and the passionate sounds of applause.

At last the report was over. Then Martov got the floor. Crooked and dishevelled, he looked very much 'the village idiot' as he demanded a peaceful resolution to the conflict, his bloodless, trembling hand on his hip. Limp applause followed from his supporters; a few of the 'old Bolsheviks' clapped from the gallery, throwing their arms wide.

Then my turn came to speak, in the name of the fraction.

It was difficult to begin. I felt that in the face of the

accomplished fact of the revolt all our former considerations and caveats were rendered quite meaningless. They had all been relegated to the past by the very fact of the revolt. And even if our forebodings should prove to be correct, at this moment of universal joy and jubilation for the people gathered here, from the front line and from all corners of our land, for their first holiday, for the first day of 'their' revolution, it would be a crime to cast the slightest shadow on this event . . . . Let the evil day come when our forebodings would come true; but at least for them this day had happened — it was theirs. And therefore, I felt that while this day lasted — my truth was a lie!

It was difficult to speak under these circumstances. But, nevertheless, speak I did. I said that from the moment that the Congress of Soviets opened, full sovereignty belonged to it and it alone. I said that now was not the time to judge the merits of what the Petrograd Executive Committee had undertaken, when it made the decision to blow down the Provisional Government's house of cards on its own initiative, without consulting this Congress. But all further developments must take place under the control of this Congress. I therefore proposed that the Petrograd Revolutionary Military Committee be placed under the authority of a body whose staff would be chosen immediately from among the members of our Congress . . . . And, pending this, in view of the total lack of fighting capability displayed by the former Provisional Government, the majority of groupings within the Socialist-Revolutionary Party, in whose name I was speaking, proposed to stop all military action immediately. The decisions which now faced us were too grave, too important to be taken against the disturbing background of the booming guns.

Trotsky picked up this theme. 'I don't believe that the sound of gunfire bothers anyone. On the contrary! It helps speed the work along.' As for the proposal itself, the Bolsheviks have nothing against its being included in the day's protocol.

Then came the turn of the old 'Tauride' factions. And the

debate of 'March' with 'October' began. Khinchuk spoke for the Mensheviks, and Gendelman for the Right Socialist-Revolutionaries. They both protested against 'the crime which had been committed against our Motherland and the Revolution'.

Meanwhile the air outside the old walls was trembling with artillery fire. The high, stately windows of our hall reverberated, in an alarming fashion, in rhythm to the shots.

Party declarations are always, ideologically speaking, merely preludes. They are always followed by the rattling of sabres.

'In the name of the front-line group of this Congress,' the chief centurion of the Right, Kuchin, yells from the podium, frowning and puffed up, 'I wish to declare categorically that the front is totally opposed to this usurpation of power.'

'He's from the brass,' the contemptuous whisper made its way around the floor. 'The General Staff sent him.' Kuchin was then roundly booed.

'Who sent you? You can tell a bird by its feathers, and we know what sort of bird you are.'

But Kuchin confidently threw back his shoulders and straightened his back, as if to challenge the hostile audience. 'I have been sent to this Congress as the representative of all the fronts and armies. And, speaking in the name of the following army committees, the 2, 3, 4, 5, 6, 7, 8, 9, 10, 11, and 12, plus the Special Army's and the Caucasus Committees' — at this point he raised his voice to its highest register, in a distinctly threatening manner — 'I wish to say that the front-line groups disclaim all responsibility for this reckless adventure, and will now boycott the Congress. From this moment on the theatre of war is here.'

From beyond the colonnades comes the energetic sound of whistling, showing the crowd's displeasure. Nevertheless, it seemed as though a sudden cloud had passed momentarily over the brightly lit assembly hall . . . .

'The Second . . . the Third . . . the Fourth . . . the Special Army . . . .'

Kamenev, sensitive as ever to the crowd's mood, immediately sends a sailor from the *Aurora* up on stage. He had been standing by the podium, shifting his weight from one foot to another, for quite a while.

Anyone who saw our sailors in those far-off revolutionary days knows the profound impression which they created anywhere they went. Their energetic figures exuded the very essence of freedom — their curt gestures and simple words cut through the air like knives. And so it was now. The auditorium shook with cries of welcome as soon as the sailor's broadshouldered, hairy-chested figure appeared on the platform. Frantically, almost as if to exorcise the dark spirit which had been called up by Kuchin's words, the Congress reached out its arms to this living symbol of the triumphant revolt . . . 'Long live the revolutionary fleet!'

'The Winter Palace is sinking fast. The *Aurora* is shooting at it almost point blank.'

'Oh no!' Twisting his hands and moaning, the pale Abramovich, who is standing at the sailor's feet, lets out a cry of despair.

And, in reaction to this piteous wail, with a generous and spontaneous gesture, the sailor comforts him, adding in a stage whisper, trembling with suppressed laughter, 'We're shooting blanks!'

Blanks is all they deserve, those ministers and ladysergeants . . . .

But, once again, with an ominous hiss, the joyous mood of the audience is shattered by new declarations coming from the Right. Abramovich, representing the Bund, hysterically calls upon the Congress to move to the Winter Palace, where a group of Bundists has decided to 'perish alongside the Provisional Government'. Both the Mensheviks and the Right Socialist-Revolutionaries, who had already split off from us, as well as a few other small groups, declare their intention of leaving the Congress.

The threats became ever sharper and more brazen. They

invoked 'the front' and 'the righteous anger of the people' which was 'inevitable . . . in the context of this mad and criminal step'. . . this comes from the SRs.

I didn't know if they themselves believed the things they were saying — but they were definitely gibing at us: 'Laugh, laugh. Your triumph will be short-lived! Is not the fact that Kerensky managed to elude the roadblocks and armoured cars of the Revolutionary Military Committee indicative of things to come? He alone, of all the Provisional Government ministers, he alone escaped: the only one whom it was imperative to arrest. And while you are amusing yourselves here with your applause and your catcalls, he is already marching towards Petrograd, already approaching its walls, at the head of front-line troops, loyal to the Provisional Government, hurrying to save the Revolution.'

'The Second . . . the Third . . . the Special Army . . . how many did Kuchin list? Would you like me to remind you? . . . . In the suburbs alone — in Gatchina, Peterhof, and Krasnyi — Kerensky has 40,000 bayonets at his command. And you? — Look around. Tally up your strength.'

And, once more, as if to parry this psychological blow, which had already begun to dim the enthusiasm of the more timid souls among us, Peterson, the Latvian rifleman, ascended the podium. Calm, ramrod-backed and big-boned, his figure, clothed in a soldier's khaki, seemed to be made of muscles and tendons alone, as if totally lacking in nerves. His presence meant that the Latvian regiments had begun to move from the front! They were already marching straight towards the rear of Kerensky's troops. That means that before he has had time to gather his support, scattered during the course of his flight, this would-be dictator will find himself between two fires . . . if he isn't already there . . . .

For — already crowding up to the podium, at the quiet call of Kamenev — here come representatives from the Gatchina and Tsarskoe Selo garrisons. They will form a live barrier between the 'pretender' and his reinforcements — as they had during the overthrow of the tsarist regime. Their garrisons have taken an oath on this.

And, once again, everything is sweetness and light in the auditorium. Dragging their feet in mourning, crushed, a trickle of Socialist-Revolutionaries and Mensheviks leave the room. 'March' has left us. . . .

Behind the platform on which the podium stands, leaning against a still damp, newly whitewashed wall, I could see the forlorn figure of Martov. He was dimly gazing through his crooked pince-nez at the cigarette strewn floor; he was still waiting, stubbornly and naïvely, for his turn to speak.

But, instead of him, we got the decisive news that the Winter Palace had fallen. All the members of the Provisional Government had been arrested and taken to the fortress. Mob justice was avoided — both the ministers and the cadets were safe and sound.

Martov's supporters hurriedly shake the dust of the hall from their heels . . . no doubt catching up with the Bundists and Socialist-Revolutionaries as they go. Our fraction leaves for consultations. I take my place on stage, once again, at the Presidium table.

But, actually, what was there to discuss? Our road was clear. At this critical moment the Party, down to its last man, had to maintain its links with the people, not daring to step back even an inch. And if, as we all expected and knew, this night would split Russia into two mortally inimical and warring camps — why, we would not be revolutionaries if we did not know where our place was in the struggle. For better or for worse, the die was cast, the bow was drawn: whoever jiggled the archer's elbow would be a traitor, and it was too late to change the target. . . .

Only one thing was certain, the true believer alone could lead at times like these. Therefore, if someone did not believe in the correctness of the Bolsheviks' predetermined road — then it was his duty to voluntarily step down from the helm and join the ranks of ordinary rowers. That was how I saw my own position, as I listened to the ensuing debate. . . .

And that is exactly what I said, during a farewell speech in which I congratulated the fraction upon its decision, put through by an overwhelming majority, to remain at the Congress.

A gloomy dawn was breaking — it was around six o'clock in the morning — when the Congress accepted the declaration 'for the workers, soldiers and peasants'.

Guided by the will of the overwhelming majority of the workers, soldiers and peasants, guided by the victorious Petrograd revolution, which has been brought about through the efforts of the Petrograd workers and garrison, the Second All-Russian Congress of Workers' and Soldiers' Soviet Deputies now takes the government power into its own hands.

The Provisional Government has been overthrown. Most of its members are already under arrest.

The Soviet government proposes to all peoples that a democratic peace be implemented immediately, and that a ceasefire take effect on all fronts. It guarantees the transfer of all lands belonging to the nobility, to the monasteries, and to the royal family, without indemnity or compensation, to peasant committees. It promises to defend the rights of the soldier by carrying through a full democratization of the army. It promises to ensure workers' control over production. It guarantees the timely convocation of a Constituent Assembly. It guarantees bread delivery to the cities and the delivery of basic staples to the countryside. It guarantees the right of self-determination to all the nations living on Russian territory . . . .

The Congress declares all local power now to be in the hands of the Soviets of Workers', Soldiers' and Peasants' Deputies, who will be the guarantors of revolutionary order.

The Congress calls upon the soldiers in the trenches to be steadfast and alert. The Congress of Soviets is certain that the revolutionary army will defend the revolution from all imperialist attempts at encroachment, until the new government achieves its goal of a democratic peace . . . .

Soldiers, workers, and professionals, the fate of both the revolution, and a democratic peace is in your hands. Long live the Revolution! . . .

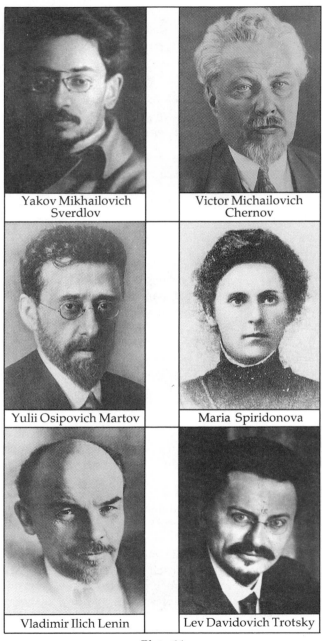

| Yakov Mikhailovich Sverdlov | Victor Michailovich Chernov |
| Yulii Osipovich Martov | Maria Spiridonova |
| Vladimir Ilich Lenin | Lev Davidovich Trotsky |

*Plate 11*

# THE
# FIFTH
# DAY

## The Day of the
## Constituent Assembly

5 January 1918

During the whole of our first revolutionary year, no day passed more quietly than the day of the Constituent Assembly. Perhaps this was because we never knew, as we got up each morning, what the new day would bring, what surprise the Fates, which had gone quite mad during these last months, would toss in our faces. But this red-letter day, which had been circled so long ago on our calendars, was 'doomed' from the start; even the Fates were chained by the iron logic of history. One could expect no surprises on this day. No more than one expects surprises when 'relics', in general, are exhumed.

And truly, by January, 1918, the Constituent Assembly had become a relic.

From that first day in October, the new Soviet regime had been wrapped in the stormy atmosphere of rising strife — civil strife, class strife, carried to a point at which any form of reconciliation was inconceivable. What we had expected all along took place — in answer to the challenge posed by the October programme the old world mobilized all of its reserves, down to the last social invalid, hobbling along on his crutches. And, in the face of the problems posed by this battle, all other problems, desires, and thoughts were pushed aside, into the background.

And so, at the very dawn of this struggle, during the first, most fiery moment of unleashed class hatred — came the date for the Constituent Assembly.

Only a few months before, when we still had not stepped beyond the pale, this Assembly, which had been the dream of revolutionary democracy for such a long time, would have been assured a decisive role in the fate of our country. But now, when 'an understanding between classes' was no longer feasible, when there was no longer any force in the whole Russian land which could re-establish 'civil' peace, which could blend together, once again, no matter with what misgivings, the world of labour with the world of capital, or at least, throw up a bridge from the new world to the old — what possible significance could this Assembly have, since any decisions it could take would be ignored equally by both embattled camps? For if the Assembly should decide, contrary to all expectations, in favour of labour, the bourgeoisie would protest, while if it should favor the bourgeoisie, the labouring people would reject its decision. There was no 'middle ground' here; the abyss separating the classes had opened up too radically to be bridged . . . .

Is it any wonder then that those very same workers and soldiers who ten months ago demanded the immediate convocation of the Constituent Assembly as the surest, and least harmful means for the reconstruction of a new Russia — as one of their basic revolutionary aims — should now turn, and with equal conviction, in the name of that same revolution, tell the adherents of the Assembly: 'You're too late' (S. Mstislavsky, 'From the February Revolt to the Constituent Assembly', *The Banner of Labour*, No.111, 5 January 1918).

Under these circumstances the Constituent Assembly was helpless, and totally incapable of making decisions. Politically, it was already quite 'dead'. And so, how could one have expected any 'surprises' from a corpse?

It's true that this corpse did have living heirs. But their words, gestures and deeds were very predictable, and they gave us no cause for alarm; they also had no surprises up their sleeves. All their supporters were well known to us. We knew that besides the Philistines, hissing from every corner, and the amateurishly conspiratorial Army officers, the Right Socialist-Revolutionaries — 'Masters of the Russian Land' — had no mass support, in any sense of the word. We were aware, it's true, of a vast effort at agitation which was going on in every corner of the city, in the offices, in the auditoriums — even, to some extent, in the factories — with the aim of flooding the streets of Petrograd with demonstrators on the day of the Assembly. We knew that quite some time before the 'official' opening, soft feminine hands were nailing new slogans to Right Socialist-Revolutionary placards; we knew of the planned attempt to organize a pilgrimage to the Tauride Palace, with the aim of bolstering the courage in the narrow chests of the preachers of social harmony . . . .

But, since these demonstrations could not possibly take on a mass character (for the true mood of the Petrograd workers and garrison was well known to us), and since they were obviously incapable of any activity more radical than flag-waving (the barricades are not the place for hysterical females) — again, this pilgrimage could bring no 'surprises' in its wake.

The same was true of the goings-on at the Tauride Palace. We knew that those 'representatives of the people' would discuss matters 'among themselves', would make some 'decisions', would cast some votes. And then they would disperse, embarrassed by their own uselessness.

That was the programme as sketched out by history ahead of time. And that is why we were getting ready for the Assembly as we would for a stage performance: we knew that this day there would be no action, as such — only spectacle.

And we were not disappointed.


Actually, the fact that the Tauride Palace was cordoned off by troops was somewhat unexpected. This led to two incidents of firing upon the demonstrators; there were both dead and wounded. The street fighting left a painful impression on us all; we had not yet been hardened to the gore of civil strife. Essentially, however, this was not really a surprise either; it fitted the mood of the day — so much so that when an investigative committee was formed to look into the incident, it was boycotted by both sides, the shooters and the shot at. This fact proved, once and for all, that the events of the 5th of January could no more be the subject of a judicial investigation than any other incidents which take place during a civil war. It was also quite in character that the Constituent Assembly itself did not react to the shootings in any way, even though news of them reached the Tauride Palace long before the actual session began . . . .

As usual, the opening session was delayed. The Socialist-Revolutionary Right, which contained the overwhelming majority of delegates, was obviously taking its own sweet time, forcing us to wait. As for us, since we were expecting a spectacle, we really had nothing to discuss among ourselves.

The impression of a stage performance was heightened by the appearance of the assembly hall itself. The members of the august body could not complain of neglect: everything in the hall, from the ceiling to the podium had been newly renovated. The platform, which had always been crowded in the days of the Government Duma, had been expanded into the room behind it. Behind the Chairman's desk, there now rose whole new sections of seating, forming an amphitheatre, framed in stucco wreathed columns. The funereal evergreens, without which no official place is ever complete, were prominently grouped in artistic groves about the platform. Their green tended to emphasize the red upholstery of the armchairs crowding the platform. All in all, everything reeked of dignity and respectability, of official government staterooms . . . and of bureaucratic red tape.

Let us now turn from the decorations to the actors themselves and the audience. The majority of the Socialist-Revolutionaries were dressed in what one might call appropriate style: in tightly buttoned frock-coats, with red rosettes in their buttonholes, starched and festive, radiantly clean shaven — in other words, exactly like provincials at a birthday party, or even more precisely, provincials going to Communion. Their ranks filled the Right and Central benches; between them and the Far Left sat the ethnic nationalist groups.

A few KDs huddled to one side. Next to them sat a tall, straight and mournful Tsereteli, who in his person represented 'one particular faction of the Mensheviks'.

Facing the deputies, at their feet, beyond the oak balustrade which protected the platform, sat the Bolsheviks, and some of the honorary guests. On the upper balconies, which had been reserved for the representatives of the workers and soldiers, a noisy and excited crowd hung over the hall like a grey-black cloud, occasionally glimmering with lights reflected from rifle barrels and bayonets. The contrast between this unkempt worker-soldier 'upper storey' and the dressed-up, carefully combed petit bourgeoisie and intelligentsia on the 'ground floor', was most instructive.

The Bolsheviks had been from time immemorial — if I may continue to use the language of the theatre — masters at staging crowd scenes. This was no small talent, and I do not mean to speak disparagingly of it. When one is dealing with the masses, only romantics do not take into consideration the visual aspect of the question. And isn't it significant that the enemies of the Soviet government — White, Black and Yellow — all tried very hard to mimic the Bolsheviks in precisely this field? They tried hard, but all in vain; their scenarios invariably failed with a resounding crash . . . .

In the Constituent Assembly 'scene', the Bolsheviks, as usual, had the upper hand. The spectacle, by its very style, demanded 'democratization' — and during the opening ceremonies we had so much 'democracy' that the most rabid democrat could not have wished for anything more.

All the newly-renovated and tidied up rooms of the palace were thrown open to the 'majority' of the Constituent

Assembly. They were given full freedom of the palace; there wasn't even a hint of barriers, barricades or prohibitions. One did not feel any government presence whatsoever. The Left — the Bolsheviks and the Left Socialist-Revolutionaries, who formed the 'ruling minority', as one of the Right Socialist-Revolutionaries put it — were very inconspicuous. The Right seemed to be the unchallenged masters of the Tauride Palace. The Soviet employees wandering the halls made way respectfully before the buttoned frock-coats and the red rosettes. The sentries standing at all the entrances and exits seemed to have been put there purely for show.

However, behind all the decorations, behind the scenery, one could feel the steel net drawing ever tighter around the palace. One strained to glimpse its presence in the sparks flying from the naked bayonets on the upper balcony, down to the naked bayonets of the 'honorary guard' standing at the foot of the platform. A snare hung over the assembly hall, a snare which had not been set on anyone's particular orders, but woven by life itself, positioned by the very meaning of events: one world against another, locked in deadly combat, a trap . . . .

And the 'constituent majority' clearly felt the snare; their decorum, their 'starch' merely served to underline their true anxiety all the more. One almost caught them glancing over their shoulders as they hurriedly took their places on the platform, behind desks which had been provided, almost jokingly, with neat piles of untouched note pads and sharpened pencils by the ever-considerate palace administration.

The Left had taken their places even earlier. But among them I didn't see any of their leaders; even I. M. Sverdlov was not in the hall, and he had been assigned to open the session by the Central Executive Committee of the Soviets.

Walking through a series of inner rooms towards the upper balcony, for a better view of the proceedings, I bumped into the said Iakov Mikhailovich Sverdlov in one of the side halls. Kamkov, Karelin of Left SRs and someone else from the

Bolsheviks, I don't recall who, were all standing in front of him, like orderlies before a colonel, tensely respectful and ready to fly at a word . . . .

'Iakov Mikhailovich, please go. Everyone is seated. I'm afraid that the Right may create some sort of scandal.'

'There's plenty of time,' answered Sverdlov, smiling broadly and good-humouredly as he continued to issue his instructions.

But he didn't make it in time. I was still climbing the steps to the upper gallery when I heard the horrendous din of desk tops crashing up and down, of shouts and piercing whistles in the hall immediately caught up and amplified by the gallery. When I walked into the box, I could see a large, heavy, elderly man, who looked like a member of the provincial gentry, standing on the platform behind the chairman's desk. He was vainly attempting to speak, his hands moving in time to his Adam's apple. The Left, whistling like mad and crashing their desk tops, completely drowned him out. His supporters among the Socialist-Revolutionaries, meanwhile, were applauding as hard as they could. Everyone in the assembly hall was standing.

Taking advantage of Sverdlov's absence, the 'majority' had attempted to open the session without permission, delegating this task by right of seniority to the deputy Shvetsov. But, in the din, he never could find an appropriate moment to utter the ritual phrase. The shouting match had already lasted several minutes, and was growing ever louder in the process. Tension was also increasing. Several of the more 'spontaneous' comrades from the Left had climbed the platform and surrounded our 'doyen', who was helplessly but — to give him his due — good-naturedly patting the chairman's bell, without daring to ring it. It seemed that one more instant, and they would grab Shvetsov by the shoulders . . . . From the benches of the Right Socialist-Revolutionaries, a group of his supporters was already hurrying to his rescue, madly applauding as they ran.

Suddenly, from behind the group on the platform, the

broad-shouldered figure of Sverdlov appeared. He exuded confidence. As always he wore an unbuttoned leather jacket, tossing back his unruly hair with a jerk of his head. Sverdlov walked up to the table, and smiling calmly, took the bell from Shvetsov's hand. The whistles from the Left and the galleries were transformed into thunderous applause. Shvetsov gave a last hurried wave, shouted something, and descended heavily from the stage. The press of people around the chairman's table evaporated. Sverdlov now stood alone, confidently leaning on the heavy handle of the bell.

The assembly quietened down. The deputies who had left their seats now hurriedly returned to them.

'I have been entrusted by the All-Russian Central Executive Committee of the Soviet of Peasants', Soldiers' and Workers' Delegates to open this session of the All-Russian Constituent Assembly.'

On the Left benches they start singing the International. The boxes start humming, voices blending, tentatively finding the right pitch. Awkwardly, uncertainly, looking at each other for support, the Socialist-Revolutionary majority rises. They are silent: only two or three sing. Zenzinov sings like a church choir master, from behind glinting glasses. Chernov, jumping up from his seat, and facing the fraction, nervously signals to them with his hands and head. Then, opening his mouth demonstratively wide, he conducts in rhythm to the measured cadences of the hymn. But they remain silent . . . . Perhaps they don't feel like singing? Perhaps they simply never learned the words?

'The Central Executive Committee assumes that the Constituent Assembly will support it in the struggle of the exploited and oppressed classes, who rose against their exploiters in October . . . .'

The even monotone cuts sharply through the silence. Sverdlov continues to read off the points which the Central Executive Committee feels that the Constituent Assembly should put on its agenda — 'since these correctly reflect the interests of the people'. He then smiled, paused, and stood silent for a moment, listening to the applause of the Left and the upper galleries, before declaring the Constituent Assembly open.

We then turned to electing a chairman.

Even this question revealed the tragedy of the constituent majority; actually, they did not have anyone to propose. We knew that there had been major debates concerning this question among the Socialist-Revolutionary Right, the result of which had been Chernov's nomination — though actually no one wanted him, and everyone criticized the nomination with the same vehemence. For some he was too far Left, for others, too far Right, and for everyone he was too much of a self-serving ass.

And here lay the party's tragedy: besides Chernov there was no one worthy, in its eyes, to 'man such a historic post'. They certainly couldn't propose Zenzinov's candidacy — he was too much the dried-up, spinsterish lady-in-waiting of 1870s populism. Avksentiev, curly-headed bon-vivant that he was, was also impossible. His peasant sympathies were so demonstrably clear that it was said he couldn't even hire a cab without doing it in the name of the 'hundred million strong Russian peasantry'. One had to admit that he was handsome enough to grace a cigar box lid; if only he had shown himself to be, in his numerous publications, at least as politically mature as, say, a Constitutional Democrat of middling intelligence . . . . And if only the workers didn't have the habit of throwing him out of political meetings in their factories, usually without allowing him to open his mouth. And if only he hadn't lost so disgracefully during the last peasant congress . . . .

Who else? Abram Gotz? Unchangingly affectionate, velvety 'Abe' — almost invisible, not once giving in to the temptation to reveal, either by word or deed, his true role of 'navigator' in Kerensky's monarchical republic . . . . Of course, if one looked at all the facts, he was by far the best candidate of the party — just as he was, to all intents and purposes, its true leader. One could at least say of him, as Jesus said of Nathaniel: 'Truly here is an Israelite who knows no cunning', a phrase totally inapplicable to Chernov.

But that of course was the whole problem. Gotz was an Israelite. And the Socialist-Revolutionary leaders, now that they were standing at the government helm — the leaders of that party which in the past had sent, without a qualm, Jewish terrorists on the road which led to hard labour or the scaffold, which founded its party slogans on Jewish thought and Jewish blood — now felt it inappropriate to nominate 'non-Russian' party members to positions of responsibility. It was hardly by chance that the party leaders forced us, the editors of the party newspaper, *The People's Task*, to print the real names of all our authors next to their pseudonymns, to make it perfectly clear that there were no Jews among us. Thus, it seemed all the less likely that the party's Central Committee should propose a non-Russian name to head the Constituent Assembly . . . .

But the pickings were very slim among the ethnic Russians. And among all these Sorokin's, Gukovsky's and Ivanov's, who were all very honest and quite nice, even Victor Chernov shone like a diamond.

Moreover, he had always been fairly flexible, our 'Minister of Agriculture'. And perhaps this flexibility, his sword-swallowing talent, could be quite useful in the complex circumstances of this 'constituent game', which so reminded me of certain games children play, for instance the 'shopping game': 'You may buy what you want, but you mustn't say "yes" or "no" and you can't buy anything in white or black.'

And so, there we had him, Chernov. The Bolsheviks and the Left Socialist-Revolutionaries proposed Maria Aleksandrovna Spiridonova as their alternative candidate. This was a totally symbolic gesture, since Maria Aleksandrovna, with her pure revolutionary spirit, was not at all a 'political' or a 'government' person. By proposing her candidacy for the chairmanship we emphasized, once again, our understanding of the

*Plate 12*   Revolutionary soldiers and sailors

Constituent Assembly's role: 'not that of an executive government organ, but one limited to a revolutionary-declarative
function' . . . . Against the political wheeling and dealing of
Chernov, we proposed the integrity and unquenchable
revolutionary fervour of Spiridonova.

The voting results were, of course, a foregone conclusion:
244 votes were for Chernov, 153 for Maria. Sverdlov, with a
calmly ironic smile, stepped down for Chernov, and Vishniak
took Smoliansky's place.

Obviously nervous, sometimes even stuttering, the new
chairman of the Constituent Assembly began his policy
speech. It dragged on for an hour. For no matter how the Left
attempted to liven things up, with its noisy catcalls, its
comments from the floor, and its whistles, his speech
remained a dead collage of bookish quotes, verse, and
pedantically turned phrases.

His attempt to make this speech completely palatable to the
Left was so obvious that even Zenzinov, normally immune to
all passions, could not suppress a shudder of revulsion.
Chernov did not once attack the Bolsheviks during that whole
long speech. On the contrary, he tried to smooth things over
as much as he could. If one discounted a few hints to the
contrary, provoked by attacks from the audience, all his main
points were consistent with the proposals voiced by Sverdlov
at the start of the Assembly, in the 'Declaration Concerning
the Rights of the Labouring and Exploited People'.

In a word, the majority who had elected Chernov were not
disappointed; he produced no surprises.

'You can't say "yes", you can't say "no"; you can't buy
black, you can't buy white.'

But the Bolsheviks were very unlikely to fall for the
transparent manoeuvrings of an enemy who was obviously
attempting to avoid an open battle. Bukharin's speech cleared
up all ambiguities on that score. An ultimatum was put before
the Constituent Assembly: they would have to choose, either
for the dictatorship of the proletariat and all of its contingent
measures as listed in the Central Executive Committee's

proposals, or for a 'wretched little bourgeois parliamentary republic', to quote Bukharin, which Chernov had been hiding behind the curtain of his eloquence all along — and which, of course, would have some contingencies of its own.

After Bukharin's militant speech, which he delivered as if at a political meeting, and which was aimed straight at the upper balconies rather than the 'dress circle', I.Z. Shteinberg's oration, despite his obviously passionate and agitated state, seemed rather pale. Shteinberg, speaking for the Left Socialist-Revolutionaries, was curt and to the point. He echoed Bukharin's sentiments at every point. 'Don't try to be clever, and don't try to wriggle out of it. Accept the declaration published by the Central Executive Committee as the programme of the Constituent Assembly, and of all further revolutionary development for Russia.'

He was followed on to the platform by Tsereteli, who was roundly booed by the Left and warmly applauded by the Right. The boos were undeserved, a spill-over from the political tensions aroused by Bukharin's speech. Tsereteli was one of the few members of the enemy camp who was always honest; this is why it was such a pleasure to cross swords with him. That day it was the same thing: in contrast to Chernov's high-wire balancing act, he calmly declared himself to be an enemy of the Central Executive Committee declaration. As in the best days of his 'February' period he spoke simply and with confidence, parrying blows from the floor as he went. Occasionally, despite the torrid atmosphere, he even forced the Left wing, which was impatiently awaiting the denouement, to pause and actually listen to his speech. And when Tsereteli, in reply to a comment made by Volodarsky, leaned down, interrupting his speech, and said in a quiet voice which was heard in every corner of the hall, 'But you, Citizen Volodarsky, you'll never be able to expiate your crimes,' the whole assembly froze in silent horror. Volodarsky himself, despite the smile on his pale lips, could not hide the shudder which passed over him. At that moment one could sense in Tsereteli's voice not anger — he could never have overcome such a din with anger — but rather a profoundly rooted belief in the truth of both his words and his judgement.

Of all the speeches given on that day within the walls of the palace, Tsereteli's was undoubtedly the best, in terms of both its content and the strength of its convictions.

When he was done the spell was broken: Severov-Odoevskii, Skvortsov and Sorokin (not Piterim, from the Right, but the Left Socialist-Revolutionary) all passed before us in a blur.

When the supply of orators had been used up, Chernov mournfully put two proposals to a vote. The first was the demand to discuss the declaration of the Central Executive Committee: this was made by the Bolsheviks. The second was Pumpiansky's counter-proposal, that the question of peace be discussed first, then land, then the government, and finally, the immunity of the Constituent Assembly and its members. There were 146 votes for the first proposal, 237 for the second. The Bolsheviks and the Left Socialist-Revolutionaries then demanded a recess, for their parties to confer in view of these results. Chernov, with the hasty courtesy he extended to all demands addressed to the presidium, immediately declared a recess.

This recess was necessary not so much for making any decision concerning 'what to do' — for a walk-out had been inevitable given the very momentum of 'the spectacle' itself — but rather to discuss how this walk-out would take place, i.e. the order in which we would leave. Logically, it seemed best for both factions to leave simultaneously, in one movement; this would have had the best theatrical effect. But politically, in terms of party rivalry, this would have been most unwise of the Socialist-Revolutionaries; they would then have completely effaced themselves before the Bolsheviks, showing themselves to be mere yes-men. On the other hand, the Bolshevik declaration had a definite governmental flavour about it; it was much too 'official' in tone, ending with the following phrase: 'Not wishing for a single moment to hide the crimes of the enemies of the people we leave this Constituent Assembly in order to transfer the final decision concerning the counter-revolutionary faction of the Constituent Assembly to the Soviet government.'

This formulation of the question was too tough for the Left Socialist-Revolutionaries.

Actually, to be precise, this is the way I had explained to myself the Left Socialist-Revolutionary decision not to participate in the Bolshevik walk-out. I did not actually participate in the negotiations. The fractions finally agreed that the Left Socialist-Revolutionaries would leave 'sometime later'.

The declaration of the Bolsheviks, which was read by Raskol'nikov after the recess, sounded like a court sentence: the deputies were pronouncing judgement on the accused, or perhaps even on the condemned. That is the way the auditorium reacted to the declaration. Chernov himself vainly attempted to preserve a dignity worthy of the chairman of such an 'important session', under the anxious gaze of his 'majority'. Without waiting for a reply, the Bolsheviks started leaving the hall, laughing and talking as they went. The 'honoured guests' followed: the members of the *narkomats*, of the Bolshevik Central Committee. Empty seats appeared on the stage and along the aisles. Already the last rows were emptying out into the left doorway, and the passageway by the podium was completely empty when suddenly — the room shuddered. The guards standing by the doorways unslung their rifles hurriedly, while their captain rushed forward, unbuttoning his holster as he ran . . . . On the benches, sprawled over the desks, several comrades were holding down Feofilaktov, a member of the Ukrainian Left Socialist-Revolutionary delegation who had attempted to fire a gun at someone in the Right faction.

It seemed that any second rifle shots would ring out. One could hear the joyous, angry sound of safety-bolts clicking up and down the upper galleries. But Feofilaktov was disarmed by his own people. Weaving, he returned to his seat, and sat down heavily, throwing his head down on his arms. The guards on the lower floor put down their rifles. And gradually, with a hollow murmur, the galleries also simmered down. The session resumed.

Shteinberg appeared once again, in the name of his party, with an ultimatum that the assembly should at least accept that part of the Central Executive Committee's proposals which dealt with the peace policy. This demand, accepted by 'the majority' in the spirit of compromise, so little resembled the Bolsheviks' behaviour that, together with the fact of the continued presence of the Left Socialist-Revolutionaries, it seemed to hearten the Right. The dress circle, obviously feeling a new lease of life, began coughing and blowing its nose. Chernov threw out his chest and gave free reign to his oratorical tendencies.

Speakers appeared from the front and back rows; further declarations followed declarations which followed earlier declarations; by factions, by nationalities and by districts.

The remaining Left Socialist-Revolutionaries obviously felt uncomfortable listening to this twittering. Even from my place in a box I could sense the anxiety rising, from the nervous gestures on the floor below me, from the increase in comments from the floor. Finally, breaking through the rhetoric, Karelin arose for another fractional declaration. He repeated, almost verbatim, the Bolsheviks' reasons for their walk-out: 'We are withdrawing because we have no wish to cover up, by our presence, that crime which in our view is being committed against the people, against the workers' and peasants' revolution, by the Constituent Assembly.'

In contrast to the Bolsheviks the Socialist-Revolutionaries, including those on the Left, were very mediocre 'stage directors': it remained unclear why exactly they had chosen to stay as long as they had, and what was the nature of the crime which their speakers had been lambasting from the moment of the Bolshevik walk-out.

One thing alone was certain: their exit sounded the last

chords of the funeral march, especially for the upper galleries. This was so clear that my neighbours to right and left expressed their sincere surprise when Chernov went on to the next item on his agenda, the discussion of a land reform bill.

'Why does he continue this farce?'

The words fall like a sad, autumnal shower among us. The galleries are slowly emptying. Night has fallen. Basically only soldiers and sailors remain up in the balconies. They are not expecting to go home: 'We'll sleep over here. No use finding our way back through the city tonight.'

Silence had fallen over the auditorium by this time. Each step echoes hollowly down the aisles, each rustle reverberates through the boxes. And an unholy terror rises palpably in the hall.

'Next I call upon . . . .'

Chernov himself has not been listening for quite a while; he himself is a prey to this same terror. He is making a discernible effort to maintain the facade of business as usual, as he shuffles papers about on his chairman's desk and pretends to study them. What could the chairman of a session possibly be studying at this time of night?

This Constituent Assembly died slowly, without agony. What they said about it having been forcefully disbanded was all vulgar nonsense! Who could possibly have wanted to raise a hullabaloo over this living relic, so fast becoming, before our very eyes, an ordinary, everyday corpse? Look now . . . one can barely see its pulse beat, hanging on a barely perceptible thread . . . . One more blow . . . . Weaker and weaker . . . . Now it will disappear altogether . . . .

A sepulchral stillness hangs over the hall. The unbearably bright electric lights which illuminate the auditorium make this stillness, this deadness, even more apparent. And, without even noticing it himself, the delegate reporting on the endless 'land reform bill' has now lowered his voice to a whisper.

'That's enough!'

Calmly and confidently, like a shot fired at point-blank range, this sailor's shout cuts through the measured whisper of the report. The deputies, instinctively ducking behind their desks, raise their eyes in fright, up to the upper galleries. And there is so much sheer animal terror in this reflex that the sailor sitting next to me, who has been leaning over the side of the balcony, spits straight down, in utter disgust, on the empty back benches.

'Hey, you . . . .'

'That's enough!'

Chernov lifts his greying head and moves the bell closer, but doesn't ring it. He understands that now is not the time to ring it. He gestures to the reader, who had momentarily faltered, to continue. He himself, affecting an air of nonchalance, lowers his eyes to the same piece of paper which has been lying there in front of him for the last several hours.

But he must raise them again almost immediately; for behind him, lightly tapping him on the shoulder, stands the captain of the guard, the sailor Zheleznyak.

The boxes quieten down. The sailor, barely bending, is saying something which we can't hear . . . .

Chernov, indignantly perplexed, falls back in his armchair.

'But . . . . All the members of the Constituent Assembly are also very tired, but no amount of exhaustion can keep us from finishing our task, from working out the land reform law which Russia is waiting for.'

Then the voice of the sailor, calmly disparaging, without any threat, rings out across the hall. 'The guards are tired. I suggest that you vacate the premises.'

Chernov leans across the table and stares directly into the eyes of his fraction. But gloomy, quiet, immobile, they seem chained to their desks — not a sign, not a word . . . . And, gazing out of the corner of his eye at the disappearing back of the captain of the guard, Chernov patters out: 'A motion has been put that this session come to a close, upon the acceptance of the land reform bill, without debate; the rest of our business can be transferred to a commission . . . .'

'What did he say?'

All around me the sailors are choking with laughter. 'What did that clown say? A motion has been put? What a joke . . . .'

Down below they are voting. The motion has been accepted. Chernov looks around: the captain of the guards is nowhere in sight.

'I also propose that an appeal be made to the civilized world . . . .'

Swallowing words, going at a very fast clip, someone grey with fear reads the appeal. The galleries are waiting patiently: the gaiety inspired by Chernov's cleverness has still not been dissipated.

The motion is carried. Zhelezniak is not here.

Just as quickly the declaration concerning 'the peace policy' is brought up. Compressing the session, Chernov is still trying to get through the planned agenda. Rustling the sheets of his report, another delegate hurries up on stage.

Once more the soldiers' faces in the boxes and on the floor turn dark and gloomy.

It is 4.30 in the morning . . . .

'That's enough!'

A shudder runs through the hall. There is a storm of shouts. We can no longer hear a word of the report, we can only follow the bloodless lips, spasmodically curling around the inaudible words.

'Get out! That's enough! That's e-nough!'

There is no longer just terror in the auditorium. There is sheer madness. I can't recognize the sailors, who were laughing just seconds ago. Their cries become ever more sharp and abrupt, their eyebrows meet threateningly over their eyes. Pupils dilated, wound tighter than a spring, painfully holding his breath, the sailor next to me slowly, silently, frees the rifle which he had been clasping between his knees.

Somewhere close by I hear the dry click of a safety bolt . . . .

'That's enough!'

Down below, almost teasingly vulnerable, one could see

the round, carefully combed heads of the delegates.

A minute, a second more . . . .

Chernov abruptly pushes back his armchair and walks away from the stage with a hurried, dancing step. The raised rifle barrels are glinting. 'What's the problem?'

'This session of the Constituent Assembly is declared closed.'

'It's about time . . . .'

Noisily and happily, as though a weight has been lifted from each heart, the soldiers call to each other, stretching and yawning, after the long and tiring session. Someone yawns with a wide open mouth, 'Watch out, don't catch any flies.'

'Well, we almost had a bunch of corpses on our hands . . .' says a young sailor, squinting his eyes as he laughs, as if to chase away the recently awakened thoughts of blood. 'A little longer and they would have made sinners of us.'

'And we wouldn't have been patted on the head for it, believe me.'

'Are you kidding? For this trash? Us Kronstadt sailors?'

In a tight bunch, pressing close to each other like a flock of sheep, the deputies are crowding around the door. Everyone tries to get through one door, the right-hand one, though the left-hand one stands perfectly clear and empty. They don't want to part company, apparently . . . .

I wait for them at the exit, in the vestibule. They walk by me in the same crowded and sheep-like mass, trying not to look around, like children in the dark.

They are all alone — there is no one in the vestibule, no one in the courtyard, no one on the street . . . . Emptiness.

Arm in arm, stumbling through the snow, walking in the middle of the street, as far away as possible from the dark doorways and fences, they walk on. The whole fraction, together. Up Tauride Prospect. In silence. Frightened. Helpless . . . .

And hurrying past them I hear Zenzinov (I recognize his voice) saying to his neighbour as he gloomily shuffles his galoshes through the snowdrifts, 'Well honestly, you must admit, we behaved with dignity.'

Thus exited the last, wavering shades of the February Revolution . . . .

*Petersburg-Moscow, 1917—1918*

# GLOSSARY

*Abramovich, Rafail Abramovich (1880—1963)*
Prominent member of the Jewish Workers' League (Bund) and a
leading member of the right wing of the Menshevik party. In 1917
Abramovich was a member of the Menshevik Central Committee
and trade union and other social organizations.

*Aleksandrovich, Grand Duke Michael (1878—1918)*
Brother of Nicholas II. Michael entered into negotiations with
leading Duma members in February 1917 and was considered a
possible constitutional monarch.

*All Russia Officers' Union*
Organization of army officers sympathetic to the Socialist Revolutionary Party during the 1905 revolution.

*All Russian Congress of Workers' and Soldiers' Soviet Deputies
(Congress of Soviets)*
National meeting of delegates from local Soviets of Workers' and
Soldiers' Deputies. The First Congress, which met from 3 to 24 June,
was dominated by moderate socialist parties and a Central
Executive Committee controlled by them was elected. The meeting
of the Second Congress took place in October. This time the
Bolsheviks were the single largest party, followed by the left
Socialist Revolutionaries. The Congress approved the Bolshevik
seizure of power and elected a Central Executive Committee under
Bolshevik control.

*Avksentiev, Nikolai Dmitrievich (1878–1943)*
A leading member of the right wing of the Socialist Revolutionary party. In 1917 Avksentiev was a member of the Executive Committee of the Petrograd Soviet of Workers' and Soldiers' Deputies, Chairman of the All Russian Soviet of Peasant Deputies and from July to August Minister of Internal Affairs in the Provisional Government.

'Banner of Labour'
The Socialist Revolutionaries' party newspaper in 1917.

*Black Hundreds*
Term applied to a number of extreme Russian nationalist movements between 1900 and 1917, the most prominent being the Union of the Russian People which was notorious for its participation in pogroms against Jews and violence against socialists and liberals.

*Bogdanov, Boris Oleivich (1884–    )*
A Bolshevik leader earlier, in 1917 a prominent member of the Menshevik party. In 1917 Bogdanov was a member of the Central Executive Committee elected by the First All Russian Congress of Soviets.

*Bukharin, Nikolai Ivanovich (1888–1938)*
A prominent member of the Bolshevik party. In 1917 Bukharin was a left wing member of the Bolshevik Central Committee and a member of the Executive Committee of the Moscow Soviet.

*Bund*
Jewish Socialist party allied in 1917 to the right Mensheviks.

*Central Executive Committee (TsIK, later VTsIK)*
The permanent committee of the nationwide All Russian Congress of Workers', Soldiers' and (at a later stage) Peasant Deputies. After October 1917, played the role of the Soviet parliament.

*Chernov, Victor Mikhailovich (1873–1952)*
Leader of the right wing of the Socialist Revolutionary party. In 1917, from February to August, Chernov was a member of the

presidium of the Petrograd Soviet of Workers' and Soldiers' Deputies and Minister of Agriculture in the Provisional Government from May until August, when he resigned over the failure to implement land reform.

*Chkheidze, Nikolai Semionovich (1864—1926)*
A leading member of the right wing of the Menshevik party. From February to August 1917 Chkheidze was chairman of the Petrograd Soviet of Workers' and Soldiers' Deputies, till he was replaced by Trotsky, and chairman of the Central Executive Committee elected by the First All Russian Congress of Soviets.

*Congress of Soviets*
See All Russian Congress of Soviets.

*Constitutional Democrat (KD)*
Member of the Constitutional Democrat party (Kadets), the main liberal party in Russia, formed in 1905. In 1917 the Constitutional Democrat party was the dominant party in the Provisional Government. As the political scene polarized, especially after some Constitutional Democrats had supported Kornilov, they became increasingly unacceptable as coalition partners to the socialists.

*Dan, Fiodor Ilich (1871—1947)*
Prominent member of the right wing of the Menshevik party. Dan was a member of the Central Executive Committee elected by the First All Russian Congress of Soviets and on its behalf opened the Second All Russian Congress.

*Democratic Conference*
Conference of socialist parties held between 14 and 22 September 1917, after Kornilov's march on Petrograd, to debate future relations with the Provisional Government.

*Duma ( also State Duma )*
The feeble tsarist parliament, elected by a highly restrictive electoral system.

*Executive Committee*
The standing committee of the Petrograd Soviet of Workers' and Soldiers' Deputies, initially chaired by Chkheidze after the Bolshevik electoral advance. The chairmanship was later taken over by Trotsky.

*Filippovskii, Vasilii N.*
Army officer and leading member of the left wing of the Socialist Revolutionary party. In 1917 Filippovskii was a member of the Executive Committee of the Petrograd Soviet of Workers' and Soldiers' Deputies and played an important role in organizing resistance to Kornilov in August.

*Gendarmes*
The tsarist political police whose responsibilities included investigation of revolutionary organizations and dealing with mass worker and peasant movements.

*Gotz, Abram Rafailovich (1882—1940)*
In 1917 Gotz led the right wing of the Socialist Revolutionary party in the Petrograd Soviet of Workers' and Soldiers' Deputies and was deputy chairman of the Central Executive Committee elected by the First All Russian Congress of Soviets.

*Guchkov, Aleksander Ivanovich (1862—1936)*
Industrialist and leader of the conservative Octobrist party. From March until May 1917, when he resigned, Guchkov was Minister of War in the Provisional Government. In August he supported Kornilov's march on Petrograd.

*Ivanov ('Iudich'), General*
Made his name as commander of punitive units during the 1905—7 revolution. In February 1917 he was ordered by the Tsar to command the loyalist forces sent to Petrograd from the front to suppress the revolution.

*Ivanov (Ivanov-Razumnik) Razumnik Vasilievich (1878—1946)*
A historian of the Russian intelligentsia who joined the Socialist Revolutionary party in 1917.

*July Days*
Large-scale disorders involving soldiers, sailors and workers in Petrograd from 3 to 4 July 1917. Some Bolshevik organizations encouraged the masses in the hope that they would overthrow the government. Despite the much more cautious attitude of most Bolshevik leaders, the July Days were followed by repression against the party which forced Lenin into hiding in Finland.

*Kamenev, Lev Borisovich (1883—1936)*
Prominent member of the Bolshevik Central Committee. After Kamenev returned from exile in Siberia in March 1917 he consistently took a moderate line and opposed Lenin's call for an armed uprising. At the Second All Russian Congress of Soviets Kamenev was elected chairman of the Central Executive Committee but resigned shortly afterwards in support of a coalition with moderate socialist parties.

*Kamkov, Boris D. (1885—1938)*
A leader of the left wing of the Socialist Revolutionary party. After October 1917 a member of the Council of People's Commissars.

*Kapelinsky, N. U.*
Prominent Menshevik Internationalist active in the Petrograd workers' co-ops. Kapelinsky became a member of the Executive Committee of the Petrograd Soviet of Workers' and Soldiers' Deputies in February 1917.

*Karelin, Vladimir Aleksandrovich (1891—1938)*
A leader of the left wing of the Socialist Revolutionary party. After October 1917 a member of the Council of People's Commissars.

*Kerensky, Aleksander Fedorovich (1881—1970)*
Leader of the Labour Fraction (Trudoviki) in the Duma. In February 1917 Kerensky was deputy chairman of the Petrograd Soviet of Workers' and Soldiers' Deputies but resigned to become Minister of Justice in the Provisional Government. After the July Days Kerensky replaced Lvov as Prime Minister.

*Khabalov, General (1858—1924)*
In February 1917 commander of the Petrograd Military District. Khabalov was replaced by Kornilov in March.

*Khinchuk, Lev Mikhailovich (1869—1944)*
A prominent Menshevik active in the trade unions and co-ops. In 1917 Khinchuk was chairman of the Moscow Soviet and led the walk-out of the right wing of the Menshevik party at the Second All Russian Congress of Soviets.

*Kornilov, Lavr Georgievich (1870—1918)*
General in the Russian army. In March 1917 Kornilov was appointed commander of the Petrograd Military District and was promoted to Supreme Commander in Chief in August. At the end of

August, Kornilov led a military mutiny which failed when the Provisional Government and Petrograd Soviet of Workers' and Soldiers' Deputies rallied their forces.

*Kronstadt*
Kronstadt Island was a major base for the Baltic Fleet less than thirty kilometres from Petrograd. The Kronstadt sailors had strong revolutionary traditions and in 1917 Kronstadt sailors were prominent in the July Days and in the October armed uprising.

*Labour Fraction of the Duma (Trudoviki)*
The Labour Fraction was a loose parliamentary grouping of mainly peasant deputies in the Duma which stood between the Constitutional Democrats and the socialist parties. Their most prominent spokesman in February 1917 was Kerensky.

*Latvian Regiments*
Soldiers from the Baltic country of Latvia serving in the tsarist army were among the firmest supporters of the Bolsheviks in 1917.

*Lenin, Vladimir Ilich (1870—1924)*
Leader of the Bolshevik party. Lenin was in exile in Europe from 1907—17 from where he vigorously opposed the First World War. In April 1917 he returned to Petrograd and persuaded the Bolshevik party to reject any co-operation with the Provisional Government and moderate socialists, adopt the slogan 'All power to the Soviets!' and prepare for an armed uprising.

*Lunacharsky, Anatolii Vasilievich (1875—1933)*
Before 1917, in exile in Europe; member of a Bolshevik faction which after 1907 opposed Lenin. In 1917 he rejoined the mainstream party. People's Commissar for Education in October 1917.

*Lvov, Prince Georgi*
Before 1917 leader of the *zemstvo* movement, organs of limited local self-government in opposition to the tsarist government. In March 1917 Lvov became Prime Minister in the first Provisional Government coalition till he resigned in July in protest at the leftwards drift of the revolution and was replaced by Kerensky.

*Martov, Yulii Osipovich (1873—1923)*
Leader of the Menshevik Internationalists. Martov, with Lenin, was

one of the founders of the Russian Social Democratic and Labour Party.

*Menshevik Internationalists*
The left wing of the Menshevik party led by Martov. In 1917 the Menshevik Internationalists agreed with the Bolsheviks in opposing the war and rejecting cooperation with the Provisional Government.

*Mensheviks*
At the Second Congress of the Russian Social Democratic and Labour party in London in 1903 the party split into Bolsheviks and Mensheviks. The Mensheviks advocated a less centralized and more broadly based form of party organization. In 1917 the majority right wing of the Menshevik party supported cooperation with the Provisional Government but rapidly lost popular support.

*Miliukov, Pavel Nikolaievich (1889—1943)*
Leader of the Constitutional Democrat party. Miliukov was Foreign Minister in the Provisional Government from March until May 1917, when he resigned after popular indignation at his support for tsarist war aims.

'Narkomat' *(People's Commissariat)*
Name given to government departments after the October Revolution. The Bolshevik leadership considered that 'ministry' sounded too bureaucratic and on Trotsky's suggestion adopted the name 'People's Commissariat'.

*Nekrasov, Nikolai V.*
Leading Constitutional Democrat. In March 1917 appointed Minister of Transport in Provisional Government. Subsequently Deputy Prime Minister to Kerensky.

*Nicholas II (1868—1918)*
Last Russian Tsar. Acceded to the throne in 1894. On 15 March 1917 Nicholas abdicated and on 21 March was arrested in Tsarskoe Selo and later sent to Tobolsk in Western Siberia.

*Octobrists*
Conservative party, so called because they were prepared to accept the Tsar's 'October Manifesto' in 1905 — in contrast to the

Constitutional Democrats who demanded greater constitutional liberties. Before February 1917 they were a dominant party in the Duma, with Guchkov and Rodzianko as their leaders, but they rapidly lost support thereafter.

*Peasant Deputies Conference (All Russian Congress of Peasant Deputies)*
National meeting of delegates from local Peasant Soviets held from 4 to 28 May. Although the Congress was politically dominated by the Socialist Revolutionary Party Lenin's speech on 22 May, when he called on peasants to take over landlords' land without waiting for permission from the government, had a powerful effect.

*Peter and Paul Fortress*
Fortress in the centre of Petrograd, founded in 1703 and best known as a prison for political offenders.

*Polovtsev, General Petr*
In May 1917 replaced Kornilov as commander of the Petrograd Military District. Polovtsev was forced to resign by the Central Executive Committee, elected by the First All Russian Congress of Soviets, for his actions during the July Days.

*The Provisional Committee of the State Duma*
A committee formed by leading members of the State Duma on 27 February 1917 chaired·by the Duma President, Rodzianko, representatives of political parties and Colonel Engelgardt who was appointed commandant of the Petrograd garrison. Negotiations between this body and the Petrograd Soviet's Executive Committee led to the formation of the Provisional Government on 2 March.

*Provisional Government*
Government set up in March 1917 consisting mainly of Constitutional Democrat members of the Duma. It was termed provisional because it was to hold power only until a Constituent Assembly which would draw up a constitution for Russia could be convoked. Later its majority consisted of right Mensheviks and right Socialist Revolutionaries. Failure in the war and economic crisis rapidly undermined its position and its composition changed several times before the Bolsheviks overthrew it in October.

*Raskolnikov, Fedor Fedorovich (1892—1939)*
Leading Bolshevik. In 1917 Raskolnikov was chairman of the

Kronstadt Bolshevik committee. After playing a leading role in the July Days he was arrested but was released in time to take part in the October revolution.

*Revolution of 1905*
Against the background of military defeat in the war with Japan and economic depression, widespread worker and peasant discontent broke out in 1905. Liberals made strong demands for the Tsar to grant civil rights and a representative assembly. As a response the Tsar issued the 'October Manifesto', convoked the State Duma and granted some civil liberties.

*Rodzianko, Michael Vladimirovich (1859—1924)*
Octobrist leader, Chairman of State Duma during the February Revolution.

*Shlyapnikov, Aleksandr Gavrilovich (1884—1943)*
In February 1917 leader of the Bolshevik underground organization in Petrograd and was a member of the founding group that established the Petrograd Soviet of Workers' and Soldiers' Deputies. In April 1917 Shlyapnikov became chairman of the metal workers' trade union and was appointed People's Commissar of Labour in October.

*Shturmer, B. V. (1848—1917)*
Prime Minister and Minister of Foreign and Internal Affairs at different times in 1916.

*Shulgin, Vasilii Vitalievich (1878—1976)*
Russian nationalist politician who was a member of the Provisional Committee of the State Duma in February 1917.

*Skobelev, Matvei Ivanovich (1885—1939)*
Leading member of the right wing of the Menshevik party. In February 1917 Skobelev was a member of the Petrograd Soviet of Workers' and Soldiers' Deputies and from May to August was its chairman. In April he was appointed Minister of Labour in the Provisional Government.

*Smol'nyi Institute*
Originally an educational institution for upper class girls. In August 1917 the Central Executive Committee elected by the First All Russian Congress of Soviets and the Petrograd Soviet of Workers'

and Soldiers' Deputies took over the building. The Revolutionary Military Committee of the Soviet which was responsible for organizing the October armed uprising was housed there too. The Second All Russian Congress of Soviets met there on 25 October 1917.

*Socialist Revolutionary Party*
A socialist party formed in 1901. In 1917 elections, Russia's largest single party. But, badly divided over tactics and programme, at the end of the year the left wing split and allied with the Bolsheviks.

*Sokolov, N. D.*
Socialist politician Sokolov left the Bolshevik party in 1914 because he supported the war effort. In February 1917, a member of the Petrograd Soviet.

*Soviet of Workers' and Soldiers' Deputies*
Soviets were councils elected by workers which evolved out of strike committees in 1905 into institutions which carried out important administrative functions. Soviets were revived in February 1917 but now frequently included deputies elected by soldiers as well. Peasant soviets were created somewhat later. At first they were dominated by moderate socialists although Bolsheviks began to win majorities from the end of August. The authority of the soviets was used by the Bolsheviks to legitimate their seizure of power in October.

*Spiridonova, Maria Aleksandrovna (1884–1941)*
Prominent member of the left wing of the Socialist Revolutionary party who was famous for having assassinated the Vice-Governor of Tambov in 1906.

*Sverdlov, Yakov Mikhailovich (1885–1919)*
Leading Bolshevik. In April 1917 Sverdlov was elected to the Bolshevik party Central Committee and played an active role in organizing the October armed uprising. In November 1917, chairman of the Central Executive Committee and *de facto* president of the Soviet state. In that capacity opened the Constituent Assembly in January 1918.

*Tauride Palace*
Until· March 1917 the seat of the Duma. From February to August 1917 the Tauride Palace housed the Petrograd

Soviet of Workers' and Soldiers' Deputies in the left wing (later in Smol'nyi) and to July the Provisional Government (later in the Winter Palace). The Constituent Assembly met there in January 1918.

*Tereshchenko, Mikhail*
Liberal politician and businessman. Tereshchenko was appointed Minister of Finance and then of Foreign Affairs in the Provisional Government and was arrested in the Winter Palace early in the morning of 26 October 1917.

*Third Section*
The name of the Russian secret political police from 1826 to 1880 when it was absorbed by the Ministry of the Interior; it remained a colloquial term for the political police.

*Trotsky, Lev Davidovich (1879—1940)*
Member of a small non-Bolshevik grouping that joined the Bolshevik party. Leading Bolshevik as from April 1917. Trotsky was arrested after the July Days but was released and became chairman of the Petrograd Soviet at the end of August. Chairman of the Soviet's Revolutionary Military Committee which was responsible for organizing the October armed uprising. Trotsky was appointed People's Commissar for Foreign Affairs in October 1917.

*Tsarskoe Selo*
Tsar's 'summer' residence about 24 kilometres from Petrograd.

*Tsereteli, Irakli Georgievich (1882—1959)*
Leader of the right wing of the Menshevik party. In 1917 Tsereteli was a member of the Central Executive Committee. Later appointed Minister of Posts and Telegraphs in the Provisional Government.

*Union of Liberation*
A coalition of individuals and groups in favour of the granting of civil liberties, representative government and social reform that helped create the Constitutional Democrat party in 1905.

*Volodarsky, Moisei Markovich (1891—1918)*
Prominent Bolshevik orator. Volodarsky returned to Petrograd from exile in May 1917. At the end of August he became a member of the Presidium of the Petrograd Soviet of Workers' and Soldiers' Deputies.

*Volyhn' Regiment*
An elite guards unit in the tsarist army formed in 1917.

*Winter Palace*
Tsar's residence in the centre of Petrograd. In July 1917 it became the seat of the Provisional Government until the night of 25—26 October when it was seized by Bolshevik-led soldiers, sailors and workers and the Provisional Government arrested.

*Zinoviev, Grigorii Yevseievich (1883—1936)*
Prominent Bolshevik. In April 1917 Zinoviev returned to Petrograd with Lenin. After the July Days he went into hiding with Lenin but opposed his call for an armed uprising. After October Zinoviev became chairman of the Petrograd Soviet.

*Jonathan Aves*